NEVER ENOUGH?

RON BLUE

WITH KAREN GUESS

NEVER ENOUGH?

3 KEYS TO FINANCIAL CONTENTMENT

B&H
PUBLISHING GROUP

NASHVILLE, TENNESSEE

978-1-4336-9071-6

Published by B&H Publishing Group
Nashville, Tennessee

Dewey Decimal Classification: 248.6
Subject Heading: PERSONAL FINANCE \ STEWARDSHIP \
MONEY

1 2 3 4 5 6 7 8 • 21 20 19 18 17

I want to, with humility and gratitude, dedicate this book to the Lord Jesus Christ. Apart from Him I would have nothing to live for and certainly I would have nothing of value to say. The words contained herein are based solely on His eternal and transcendent truth.

CONTENTS

Introduction

Welcome.

Welcome to this money book.

Reading a book about money is sort of like brushing your teeth as a kid. You know you need to do it and that it will provide long-term benefits, but the draw toward other things is stronger and usually wins in the battle for our attention and focus.

Having spent a lifetime counseling people about their money, I realize that it can be an unappealing topic. You're not alone if you get that strange mixture of desire and dread when you think about tackling financial goals!

So, before we even begin, I want to commend you for being willing to "enter the fray"—for being willing to pick up a book on money and turn to the first page. I'm so glad you're here.

You see . . . I believe it can be different.

I believe that you can experience deeper contentment and walk through financial decisions with more confidence. I believe that your financial life can be a place of sure-footed decision making. I even believe that your relationship with your heavenly Father can be stronger and deeper as you learn to listen to Him and integrate His wisdom into your financial decisions. In fact, I'll be bold and go so far as to say that I believe the perspectives, principles, and processes in this book will lead you toward confidence and contentment in your financial life.

So, I write this with much anticipation—excitement, even— on your behalf. I believe so deeply in the transformational power of biblical financial wisdom that I've spent an entire five-decade career sharing it with anyone and everyone who will listen, and I have seen countless men and women embrace the truths of biblical financial stewardship. As they lived as stewards, they began to experience more content, confident, and financially free lives. Biblical financial wisdom transformed my life. I believe it can transform you. I even believe that it can radically transform the world.

This is a journey we will take together, one where I simplify biblical stewardship by sharing three keys to financial contentment.

First, we will examine the power of perspective. It truly is remarkable to understand how a faith-filled and biblically oriented perspective on the intersection of God, money, and our lives changes our understanding of our financial decisions.

Then, we'll learn a few (just five!) biblical principles. Following these simple principles on how to handle our money provides clarity in places of financial confusion. They are basic, straightforward, and best of all—they work!

Finally, we'll take a look at a diagram—the pie diagram—and learn how this simple picture can help us understand and prioritize our financial decisions in the face of so many options, priorities, and pressures.

However you come to this book—with excitement, dread, shame, hope, fear, or anticipation—welcome. I'm so glad you're here.

1

A New Money Story

Y ou have a numbers story.

Maybe it's a story of driven, hard work—years of sustained effort to intentionally shape your financial future.

Maybe your story is one of powerful generosity—love for the marginalized, marked by an open hand and a willing checkbook.

Perhaps it's a story of lifelong struggle—consistently overcoming the factors that made your financial future difficult from the day you were born.

Many people's numbers tell a story of "never enough"—anxiety over what-ifs and regret over should-haves that drive the next financial decision.

Maybe your numbers—your finances—really tell a deeper story about YOU. I believe that they do, and I want to take a journey with you to unpack both your numbers and your story. I want to show you what's possible.

It is possible to have a numbers story that speaks confidence to the world around you. Because God's Word speaks straightforward financial wisdom, you really can make decisions from a place of firm footing without holding an advanced degree in finance.

It is possible to have a numbers story that is marked by contentment. You can be satisfied—deeply so—in your current financial situation, even while boldly pursuing "next steps" for savings, debt payment, and lifestyle goals.

It is even possible to have a numbers story that is marked by good communication with your spouse and family. You can learn how to approach financial decisions from a perspective-based level, working to align your goals while standing on the common ground of shared beliefs.

I have a numbers story, too, and there was a moment in time when I woke up to the fact that all of our stories are pretty similar—whether we have a lot or a little.

Mud Huts and Money

I grew up in the Midwest. As the son of an immigrant mom and a farmer-turned-factory-worker dad, my roots are humble. My parents worked hard to ensure that our family made it into the American middle class during my growing-up years.

As a young man, I was pretty enamored with new stuff (as most young men are). My love for baseball gloves turned into a love for clothes and cars, which then morphed into a love directed at a new house and a country club membership.

From my perspective, I was a normal, red-blooded American child of the 1950s. The pursuit of stuff—materialism—was woven into my DNA. I never had quite enough to satisfy the longings of my heart.

When I became a Christian in my thirties, God led my wife and me to make some radical decisions. These decisions would impact everything from career and location to family and home. My service shifted from small business owners through my thriving CPA practice to African pastors through leadership training events in places like Kenya and South Africa.

Needless to say, meetings in Sub-Saharan Africa were a bit different than meetings in suburban Indianapolis.

On one of my visits to Kenya, Pastor Daniel invited me to his home. Pastor Daniel lived with his wife and several children in a mud hut on the edge of a village. He and I sat in his yard, near his chickens, as we talked. We discussed the specific challenges he faced as he shepherded his congregation. While we talked, I couldn't help but notice the drastic lifestyle differences between us . . . but there was something that also felt so familiar. The youngest of his children was playing nearby in the dirt with a D battery, thoroughly engaged in whatever imaginative scenario the battery represented. I found myself thinking about the imagination-boosting options available to my children on a Saturday morning (cartoons, Big Wheels, a sandbox, and a swing set, to start!) compared to his daughter's "toy" battery. I was a bit chagrined.

As we chatted, I asked Pastor Daniel to share with me the biggest hindrance to the spread of the gospel in his part of the world. Without hesitation he answered, "materialism."

What!?

How?!

I had to ask.

"You see," he said, "if a man has a mud hut, he wants a stone hut. If he has a thatched roof, he wants a tin roof. If he has one room, he wants two rooms."

Apparently, and much to my surprise, materialism is a disease of the heart that affects all people—it is not simply a disease suffered only by the "haves." That day, I realized that the "haves" exist in every cultural context, no matter the relative poverty level.

My young mind was blown! From that moment on, I read Jesus' teachings about money with a new set of lenses. I realized that Jesus talked so much about money because the issues money creates are not just issues of the wealthy; they are issues of humanity. Every person struggles with issues of money—materialism, greed, envy, control, stinginess, impulsivity, fear, and comparison.

Money is a great revealer of the heart. I often say that if you give me your bank statement, I can pinpoint you where you struggle and where you are free. I can identify your priorities and your goals. I can see what you love by looking at your checkbook. Many times, a checkbook will even show me what you fear. This trend is unsettling, but very true.

> Money is a great revealer of the heart.

Jesus Himself famously said, "For where your treasure is, there your heart will be also" (Matt. 6:21).

Where Is My Heart?

I once heard pastor Tim Keller give a sermon on money. He remarked that he has never had someone come to him privately to confess the sin of greed. He's had parishioners confess plenty of other sins to him, but never greed.[1]

Why? Because, collectively, we suffer from blindness when it comes to the connection between our heart and our money. We cannot see what is so close to us and what is so engrained in us. None of us think we are greedy even though we can see this problem boldly play out in the lives of others around us.

If we are all blind to the greediness that exists, what is the solution? How do we begin to see it in order to deal with it? Or, better yet, do we truly want the true nature of our heart to be revealed to us?

God knows our weakness in the area of finances and He wants to use that area of vulnerability to display His strong power in our lives. This good news—this exchange of His power for our weakness—is **the** story of the gospel. The gospel story is His vision for our blindness, His redemption for our sin, His abundant life for our dead works. Jesus is always accomplishing the good news of the gospel in the life of a Christian—even when it comes to money. Especially when it comes to money. Learning His truth about money will empower you with vision and freedom and confidence in your financial decisions.

Because God knows the inevitable overlap between our hearts and our money, He filled the Scripture with perspectives and principles about money. In His Word, He gives us all that we need to walk a path of confident stewardship. He gives us His wisdom through the Holy Spirit along with reliable lenses to evaluate our financial thinking and our financial decisions.

Our relationship with money is similar to our relationships with people. Just like in key relationships, our financial life is also fertile soil for God to work. Money provides a training ground for spiritual growth that will last into eternity.

True, Timeless, Transcendent

My wife teases me that I am not happy until I can get my main points to start with the same letter when I give speeches. Her kidding is very well deserved, but I think that devices like rhyming and alliteration are powerful, so I'll share one of my favorites with you here.

> God's Word on the topic of money is true, timeless, and transcendent.

God's Word on the topic of money is **true**, **timeless**, and **transcendent**.

First, it is **true** in that it **works**. In my career, I've worked in a variety of financial environments. I've worked on Wall Street with one of the world's largest accounting firms and in a small, private bank. I started a CPA firm that served small businesses and individuals. I have counseled thousands of Christians via a financial planning firm that I founded in 1979 and trained several thousand financial advisors who want to add biblical wisdom to their advice.

And I have interacted extensively with the public via media outlets about their financial questions.

While this litany sounds a bit like Paul's résumé run-up in Philippians about his life as a Pharisee, I will tell you that, similar to Paul, I count all these things loss in view of the amazing grace of knowing Jesus. Every word that He said about money is true, and it has transformed my heart.

When I came to Christ in the early 1970s, I was mid-career. Over time, God began to weave my vocational financial skills with the knowledge of what His Word says about money. As that intersection happened, the powerful truth of Scripture about money shined brighter and brighter. With each year that has passed, the truth of biblical financial wisdom has become more and more evident to me.

In every environment, on every financial platform that I've stood, God's principles about money in Scripture are effective. They work on Wall Street and they work on Main Street. They work for the millionaire and they work at minimum wage. Any "wisdom" about money that is successful in the world is somehow derived from the wisdom of Scripture on the same topic. What God's Word says about money is true. I've built my fifty-plus-year career on it.

Additionally, it is **timeless** in that it **remains**. Scripture's teaching on money worked in the context in which it was written and works in our context today.

When King Solomon wrote things like, "The rich rules over the poor, and the borrower becomes the lender's slave" (Prov. 22:7 NASB) or, "Wealth obtained by fraud dwindles, but the one who gathers by labor increases it" (Prov. 13:11 NASB), he was not thinking of the stock market or subprime mortgages or Ponzi schemes or low APRs. Those terms would have been entirely foreign to him!

Yet, in an era of online banking and a global economy, the principles about money remain. They are timeless. They will remain far past anything we can imagine in terms of economic trends or financial instruments because timelessness is the nature of biblical wisdom.

Finally, it is **transcendent** in that it is **reliable**. Biblical financial wisdom transcends changes throughout a lifetime. Judy and I began our married life living in a trailer that was so small, the opened ironing board took up the whole living space. Now, all these years later, we have lived in multiple homes and we have cleaned out multiple attics and basements. We have paid for college degrees, weddings, first cars, car wrecks, vacations, and so much more. Some days it seems like we have purchased insurance on our insurance. Our financial life is endlessly more complicated than it was when I was twenty-two. Nevertheless, the biblical financial wisdom I have learned and share in this book transcends each decision, each life stage, and the needs of each of the five children that have come and gone from our now empty nest. Biblical financial wisdom is reliable, no matter how my circumstances change. It is transcendent.

The Iceberg

I happen to think that the iceberg is one of the best representations in nature of the power of wisdom. Have you ever seen one firsthand? If so, you know that the beauty and grandeur of what rises above the surface is breathtaking. When a bit of ice breaks off and falls to the water below, the glorious fall makes you want to clap your hands and shout.

What I love most about icebergs, though, is that they hide exponential grandeur and beauty below the surface. Ninety percent of an iceberg sits beneath the surface of the water. What sits on top is, well, just the tip of the iceberg!

Similarly, the run-of-the-mill, cultural financial messages that we hear tend to be ten percent of the story or "tip of the iceberg" messages. Most television commercials advertising financial advice focus on the "tip of the iceberg" type questions: How do I retire early? How do I save for college? How do I get out of debt? How do I get a lower interest rate? How do I take advantage of this economy? And so on.

Biblical wisdom about money is more about what lies below the waterline. Until we understand a wise perspective and know certain principles about money, we will not be able to make confident decisions. We will not be able to be content because there will be so much below the surface that remains unknown and uncertain. Our number stories will remain tumultuous.

A journey beneath the waterline may be a new experience for you. Think of this book as a chance to be fitted with scuba gear to take you below the waterline and gain clarity and focus where there is confusion and fuzziness. We will certainly explore some "how" answers in the book, but I first want to help you with the "why" so that you have the power to make wise financial decisions in the midst of shifting life circumstances over time. Our "why" determines our "how." What we believe determines what we will do. If we have a settled understanding of biblical perspectives and principles about money, then our decisions about money will become more confident and will be rooted in a solid trust in the ultimate owner of our resources—God Himself. Isn't that wonderful?

Not long ago, I saw a powerful video that illustrates the power of acting out of "why" rather than "how." Christian comedian Michael Jr. did a stand-up routine in North Carolina. During a break in his routine, he interacted with the audience and discovered that there was a music teacher at the show. Michael put the teacher on the spot by challenging him to sing "Amazing Grace." The teacher responded to the challenge by singing a beautiful, level version of the first verse of the song, to the applause of the audience. Finding out that the man had a voice, the comedian went a step further and messed with this poor teacher in new ways. He told the teacher, "Now sing 'Amazing Grace' like your uncle just got out of jail." The music teacher rose to the occasion and practically blew the roof off of the venue with a chillingly powerful rendition of the song. By the end, people were standing and cheering and the comedian was virtually speechless. Once the teacher knew his "why," the song took on a life of its own, and it became a work of art rather than just a melody.[2]

> Our "why" determines our "how." What we believe determines what we will do.

Similarly, knowing how to make a budget or pay off debt or give responsibly is important. But when your financial actions and plans and decisions are infused with a powerful, biblically based understanding of "why," your financial life can become a life of impact, hope, confidence, and contentment. Through our time together, I pray that you will experience the reality that knowing the good news of biblical financial wisdom frees you to make outstanding financial choices from a place of heart-level conviction.

Takeaway

On that long-ago day in Africa, I realized that the connection between heart and money is universal. Regardless of my income level, God wants to use money to help transform my heart.

Consider that God wants you to understand money in a whole new light, and perhaps for the first time you'll realize:

His wisdom applies to your money.
His work in your heart is tied to your financial struggles and victories.
His Word applies to every part of your life, including money.
His "why" can inform your "how," transforming your money story.

Do you agree it's time to break down the God/Money divide? Pull up a chair to the true, timeless, transcendent wisdom of Scripture and ask the Lord to open your eyes.

BRAD'S STORY

God Provides

Brad was one of my sons' best friends when they were growing up. In school, he was sandwiched in the grade right in between my two boys and they played tennis together for many years. Our family was a fixture at the tennis courts during this season of life, and Brad was often a part of the mix. One summer, he even lived with us.

In high school, Brad had his share of close calls. He flirted with the wild side, and he encountered the subsequent heavy hand of school discipline more than once. His path wasn't the "straight and narrow," but the Lord pursued him through relationships with mentors along the way. Eventually, Brad met Jesus and looked for chances to mentor and care for people the way others had mentored and cared for him.

Today, in his late thirties, Brad is a counselor, teacher, and pastor. His impact on the men and women in his care is deep. He is one of the most insightful and genuinely caring men that I know and is a role model to many young people in his circle of influence.

Brad's high school foibles didn't happen in a vacuum. When he was in middle school, his family went through a really hard season. His parents divorced, leaving his mom to care for three boys on a teacher's salary. His mom ended up working three jobs—teaching, tutoring, and delivering papers—to make ends meet. She had a rotation of waking up a different son each night to ride her paper route with her so that she could stay awake. The financial road was challenging for their family in ways most of us who knew them didn't begin to realize. It was one of those tough situations where his mom was living and working in a fairly affluent environment, but their family circumstances conspired to leave them on the verge of financial despair, without anyone understanding the reality of their day-to-day situation.

At one point, Brad, his brothers, and his mom were kicked out of their home. They moved to an apartment but were barely making it. Brad said, "I remember my mom being so upset that she couldn't even wash our clothes" because she did not have enough money to buy detergent. The very same day of her laundry-induced breakdown, his mom went to the mailbox and found that a sample of laundry detergent had come in the mail. God had provided enough for that moment.

Grace.

Provision.

Care.

Clean clothes for three growing boys.

As Brad puts it, "A cool aspect of that to me is that no one in our family was following the Lord at that point—and yet we were cared for in a very personal way by the Lord that wasn't tied into any sense of faithfulness on our part."

The care and provision of our heavenly Father misses nothing—not even the laundry.

As we dive into the sometimes challenging reality of financial stress, change, goals, or plans, I hope you will remember that God knows your needs—down to the load of whites or darks that you have tumbling in your dryer. He is able to creatively meet you at your point of need, perhaps before you even know to ask Him. His heart is to draw each of us to Himself, with the knowledge that He is gracious in His provision and that He is the ultimate provider of all things. This is true whether we have the means to solve our current financial woes or not.

I know Brad's pastor-heart wants you to be encouraged by his small but profound money story about laundry. I hope you carry it with you as you consider the amazing grace of being known and loved by your perfect heavenly Father.

2

Who Owns It?

Recently, my daughter shared a story about a woman who was baptized at her church. The woman being baptized was a driven, high-achieving doctor. She had competed as a college-level tennis player and had become a surgeon in a very competitive field, among other things. When she began to follow Jesus, she started a very interesting daily ritual. You see, as a surgeon, she knew that when one of her patients went into surgery, they had to sign a release form saying that they trusted her as their doctor and would accept any outcome of the surgery about to be performed. After she became a Christian, the doctor began keeping a stack of "release forms to God" on her bedside table. Every morning, she signs a form when she gets out of bed, in recognition of the fact that her good heavenly Father will be working in her heart and life that day. The young doctor is intentionally surrendering to God's work each day.

Key #1: Perspective (Stewardship)

One of the greatest heart-level illusions about our money is that we have control over it. Whether we sign a money release form or not, God owns it all.

Our possessions seem like they are "ours." But the powerful assertion of Scripture is that God owns everything, whether we acknowledge His ownership or not. As Creator and Sustainer of the universe, as the One who spoke the world into being and as the One who sets eternity in the hearts of men, God owns it all.

The statement is simple, but it is revolutionary in its scope and application. If God owns it all, it changes my relationship to almost everything. If God owns it all, so many things matter in a different way than they did before.

When I believe that God owns it all . . .

My trust in His goodness grows.

My belief in His sovereignty expands.

My attentiveness to His voice sharpens.

My perspective about how much I have—my possessions, my reputation, my family, my sphere of influence, my future plans, my past healing, and more—shifts from consumption to stewardship.

My concern over other people's opinions diminishes; I now know that I play for an "audience of one."

If God owns it all, then my money matters differently. But more than that, if God owns it all, I enter a sacred and beautiful trust that extends far beyond my tithe or my year-end giving. If God owns it all, I become free to view life as a great adventure with Him, stewarding my all for His glory.

Bill and Vonette Bright's Story

Some dear friends and mentors of mine, Bill and Vonette Bright, evidenced a life of great adventure with God in ways that provided a profound testimony to the world. When I met them in 1974, I knew of their influence in the lives of college students across the world with the message of Jesus and His good news. At that time, their ministry, Campus Crusade for Christ, was having Kingdom impact via dozens of ministries that served colleges, marriages, the media, athletics, politics, the military, and more. I could see the "tip of the iceberg"—all of the lives that were being transformed by Jesus—and I was encouraged and amazed.

> If God owns it all, I become free to view life as a great adventure with Him, stewarding my all for His glory.

While serving on the board of directors for over twenty-five years, I got to know Bill and Vonette, and was increasingly encouraged and amazed by what was "beneath the waterline" of their faith and their vision. One story stands out to me as characteristic of the way that the Brights' perspective of God's ownership impacted everything in their lives. In Dr. Bright's own words, the story starts when he was a very young man running his own business in Hollywood in the early 1950s . . .

> I was in business in Hollywood and worked day and night to succeed. Like most Americans, I had that desire to build my own empire. I was the lord of my empire. In my ignorance, I had no knowledge of God, though I had been baptized when I was twelve. But I was not at all interested in church through college and graduate school and in business in Hollywood. Then one day, in the providence of God . . . I was introduced to Christ.
>
> [Vonette and I] had been married about two years when the Lord impressed us through a series of circumstances that we should surrender everything to the Lord Jesus. So we wrote out and signed a contract . . . I am a businessman by trade, so I figured that is the best way to register our commitment. So we signed that contract that afternoon in 1951. About twenty-four hours later . . . in a way that was life changing, God met with me and gave me a vision for the world, which we call Campus Crusade for Christ. So Vonette and I have known an adventure all these more than fifty-three years of marriage that is almost beyond description.
>
> First of all, had there been no contract, in my opinion, there would have been no vision. God brought us to the place

where we made total, absolute, irrevocable surrender. Then He knew He could trust us, and from there on the vision began to be implemented and still is being implemented all over the world.

From a practical point of view, we view God as someone we know we can trust implicitly. So when He led us to start this ministry, we knew He would guide us. But it is all God's doing. And literally, we view ourselves as a suit of clothes for Jesus . . . Your view of God determines everything: your lifestyle, your friends, your literature, the music you enjoy. Everything about you is influenced by your view of God . . . We have been bought with a price, the precious blood of the Lord Jesus.[3]

Bill and Vonette literally, contractually acknowledged God's ownership of all of their possessions—their very lives—and God used them in powerful ways for His Kingdom. I think the key in the Brights' story is Bill's remark, "your view of God determines everything." In his book *The Knowledge of the Holy*, A. W. Tozer said, "What comes into our minds when we think about God is the most important thing about us."[4]

Our belief about who God is and our view of His ownership will shape everything about our lives. I cannot convince you of His character or His ownership. But I can reassure you that when people truly believe God's good and sovereign ownership, their lives and the world around them are beautifully transformed.

In my career as a financial advisor to Christians, I found that the people who were the most free and confident in their financial decisions were the people who had, effectively, signed a release form to God, yielding to His will and listening for His voice. I learned that surrendering to God's ownership explodes life's possibilities rather than diminishing those possibilities. When Bill and Vonette signed their contract and gave God the rights to all they possessed, they did not impoverish themselves; rather, they turned themselves over "to Him who is able to do exceedingly abundantly above all that we ask or think" (Eph. 3:20 NKJV).

Parable of the Talents

In one of Jesus' parables, He talked specifically about the dynamic that happens when we acknowledge God as owner and ourselves as stewards in the Kingdom of God.

"Again, the Kingdom of Heaven can be illustrated by the story of a man going on a long trip. He called together his servants and entrusted his money to them while he was gone. He gave five bags of silver to one, two bags of silver to another, and one bag of silver to the last—dividing it in proportion to their abilities. He then left on his trip.

"The servant who received the five bags of silver began to invest the money and earned five more. The servant with two bags of silver also went to work and earned two more. But the servant who received the one bag of silver dug a hole in the ground and hid the master's money.

"After a long time their master returned from his trip and called them to give an account of how they had used his money. The servant to whom he had entrusted the five bags of silver came forward with five more and said, 'Master, you gave me five bags of silver to invest, and I have earned five more.' The master was full of praise. 'Well done, my good and faithful servant. You have been faithful in handling this small amount, so now I will give you many more responsibilities. Let's celebrate together!'

"The servant who had received the two bags of silver came forward and said, 'Master, you gave me two bags of silver to invest, and I have earned two more.' The master said, 'Well done, my good and faithful servant. You have been faithful in handling this small amount, so now I will give you many more responsibilities. Let's celebrate together!'

"Then the servant with the one bag of silver came and said, 'Master, I knew you were a harsh man, harvesting crops you didn't plant and gathering crops you didn't cultivate. I was afraid I would lose your money, so I hid it in the earth. Look, here is your money back.' But the master replied, 'You wicked and lazy servant! If you knew I harvested crops I didn't plant and gathered crops I didn't cultivate, why didn't you deposit my money in the bank? At least I could have gotten some interest on it.'

"Then he ordered, 'Take the money from this servant, and give it to the one with the ten bags of silver. To those who use well what they are given, even more will be given, and they will have an abundance. But from those who do nothing, even what little they have will be taken away. Now throw this useless servant into outer darkness, where there will be weeping and gnashing of teeth.'" (Matt. 25:14–30 NLT)

As I read this parable, I see a few important lessons about stewardship.

1. The Amount Is Not Important

First of all, a key in this parable is that the stewards are all given different amounts, and the amount is not important to the owner's commendation or the steward's responsibility. The exact same words are spoken to the steward with two bags and the one with five bags. God is neither condemning wealth nor commending poverty in this parable; He simply desires for those who care for His resources to do it with wisdom, courage, and faith. Whether a steward has a little or a lot, every spending decision is a spiritual decision since it is all God's money.

> Every spending decision is a spiritual decision since it is all God's money.

2. Faith Requires Action

The servant with only one bag gives into fear and does not take responsibility for what he has been given. Sometimes we know what faith would have us do with our money, but we avoid action—we have knowledge but no active faith. Often, applying biblical financial wisdom requires faith and courage on our part.

3. We Are in a Growth Process

The servants with two and five bags are "given many responsibilities" when their master returns, and He invites them to "celebrate together" with Him. Their initial stewardship opportunity prepares them for something bigger in eternity. Scripture teaches that our reward and responsibility in eternity is in direct proportion to our stewardship and growth on the earth. This life is a training ground for what is next. It is fascinating to imagine what responsibilities we will have and what celebrations we will enjoy in the economy of heaven!

Money: God's Secret Weapon

Have you ever thought about the point of money, from God's perspective? Some of you might be economics majors or finance people who spend a lot of brainpower considering the philosophical or practical point of financial systems, but I'm guessing most of us haven't spent much time thinking about the purpose of money from

God's perspective. I tend to think of money as being God's secret weapon in our lives.

We've already said that our money and our hearts are inextricably linked. Maybe that's why there are more than two thousand verses about money in the Bible. If money issues are really heart issues, God can use money to get to (and change) our hearts. I think money is His secret weapon!

God uses money in three ways: as a tool, as a test, and as a testimony.

First, God uses money (both extra money and lack of money) as a **tool** to shape our hearts. Money reveals the condition of our hearts, and we are often most vulnerable and open before the Lord when we face financial challenges. When we encounter financial struggles, we can confidently ask God, "What do You want me to learn?" We are wise to recognize that our financial situation is often the way that He grows us up in areas of contentment, gratitude, faith, and more. Our bank account is like a classroom for grown-ups, and God takes full advantage of the teachable moments!

The apostle Paul experienced times of abundance and times of need during his ministry to the early church. When he wrote to the Philippians, he shared about his financial ups and downs, remarking that he had "learned to be content" (Phil. 4:11). Like a sculptor with a chisel, God had used Paul's varying financial experiences to shape his heart toward greater contentment over time.

The second way God deploys the "secret weapon" of money in our lives is when He uses money as a **test.** Luke 16:11–12 (NIV) says,

"So if you have not been trustworthy in handling worldly wealth, who will trust you with true riches? And if you have not been trustworthy with someone else's property, who will give you property of your own?" Somehow, in God's economy, our eternal reward is tied to the use of God's resources on the earth. Mysteriously, the way we use money here on the earth is a test that prepares us for the handling of resources much more "true" in eternity. I don't pretend to understand this reality, but I believe that testing is a key function of money in our lives as Christians, from God's perspective.

Bill and Vonette Bright believed that God granted them the beauty of a vision for the ministry of Campus Crusade for Christ only after they had passed His test and surrendered their rights to their material resources to Him. As they faithfully handled their worldly wealth by putting it in proper perspective, God entrusted them with the true riches of a life of adventure on mission with Him.

Last, God uses money in our lives as a **testimony**. In Matthew 5, Jesus calls us to be salt and light. He teaches that His followers will live lives that look vastly different from the lives of others. Simply put, as God gets ahold of our hearts, it will be obvious to the world by our attitudes toward money. We will live lives that are free from fear, greed, envy, and materialism, and those around us will wonder why. The world cannot help but notice a difference.

I hope that as you read, you are getting excited about the bigger picture—the power of living as a steward and the joy of watching for what God is doing in our hearts and in the hearts of those around us as we follow Him in our finances.

Takeaway

Being a steward is an opportunity to go on an adventure with our Master. More than just knowing the "right" thing to do with our money, we get to see firsthand as He uses one of the most common, human things—our money—to accomplish His good purposes and shape us into the person He wants us to become. I realize that whether I have little or much, how I handle my money demonstrates where I place my greatest treasure. It proclaims to everyone around me that God is in control and can be trusted implicitly.

As God gets ahold of our hearts, it will be obvious to the world by our attitudes toward money. We will live lives that are free from fear, greed, envy, and materialism.

Do you acknowledge your heavenly Father's sovereign ownership and yield to it? Understanding that God owns it all is the first step on a powerful journey of stewardship!

3

Perspective Changes Everything

Do you remember the story of the twelve spies—the ones Moses sent out from the Israelites' camp to spy on the inhabitants of the Promised Land? Two of the spies—Joshua and Caleb—came back with one story: "We must go up and take possession of the land because we can certainly conquer it!" (Num. 13:30). The other ten came back singing an entirely different tune. These ten leaders of Israel, after spending forty days in the land and examining both its bounty and its population, reported, "We can't go up against the people because they are stronger than we are! . . . To ourselves we seemed like grasshoppers, and we must have seemed the same to them" (vv. 31, 33).

Look at what the ten guys said again. They said "to **ourselves** we seemed like grasshoppers, and we must have seemed the same to them." Seeing the circumstances and task before them—conquering a whole lot of really big guys across the river—caused them to see themselves as insignificant and ineffective. Their perspective was skewed, and the biggest problem about that skewed perspective was how they saw **themselves**.

Key #1: Perspective (Contentment, Wisdom, and Faith)

Sometimes when we encounter financial hurdles or when we try to communicate with our spouse about money or when we imagine our financial future in the face of today's demands, we encounter a perspective problem. We start to see ourselves as insignificant or ineffective. We begin to see the fight as insurmountable because the problems loom large.

Seeing overwhelming circumstances
Causes us to feel small (like grasshoppers)
So that the overwhelming circumstances seem bigger . . . and bigger
Until we decide we won't take on the fight.

Financial battles are no small thing. They can take us into territory requiring new habits, new priorities, and new vision. Our perspective toward our financial issues makes all the difference in the world—perspective undergirds the way we view ourselves, our problems, our future, and our chances of victory. Without a perspective that is rooted in truth, we can end up wandering in the proverbial desert for a few years or more.

We've already talked about having a stewardship perspective. Believing that God owns it all is the most fundamental perspective shift about our money that we can adopt. But I believe there are a few other key biblical perspectives that are important to have when it comes to our money. All of these perspectives are ways to reorient ourselves away from the inevitable overwhelming circumstances around us and toward the truth of God's wisdom about money. They undergird us with a firm foundation, strengthening what is under the waterline. Having these perspectives makes us strong for the financial battles that are inevitable.

Contentment: How Much Is Enough?

There is a tension in our world today. It exists somewhere in the pull between the Facebook phenomenon and the farm-to-table trend. On Facebook, we see the more, better, and shiny that our friends offer up. More vacation bliss, better family photos, shinier blogs. In the farm-to-table trend, we celebrate simplicity—the limits of what the local earth produces and the beauty that can come from hard work and creativity. We're caught between the tag lines and slogans that appeal to our narcissism and those that play on our nostalgia for something simpler. It's easy to become confused, not knowing whether to buy a whole new patio set at Costco on our way home from work or carefully handcraft porch furniture from reclaimed pallet wood ourselves.

To return to the spies analogy, it's as though we are the spies, scoping out the battle and being inundated with the conflicting messages of our culture (more . . . less . . . more . . . less . . . more). It becomes difficult to know how to stand our own ground—the ground we've been given by God to steward.

So, how much is enough? Is there a biblical perspective that will allow us to conquer this tension of mixed messages in American culture today?

In my early adulthood, I realized I had bought the lie that having more money guaranteed me success, security, and significance. I believed if I could have more money, I would automatically feel more successful, more secure, and more significant. It was revolutionary to my own financial life when I took the pressure off of money to make me feel a certain way and turned to God's truth about finding my identity in Him.

When you think about your own finances, what pressure are you putting on your financial life? What do you expect your money to do for your heart that is impossible?

I believe that the key to resolving this "more" struggle is adopting a contentment perspective. The hard truth is that the answer to the "how much is enough?" question is neither more money nor less stuff. Simply speaking, Scripture teaches that the answer to the "how much is enough?" question is what I have **right now**.

Take a fresh look with me at two familiar passages of Scripture:

Keep your lives free from the love of money and be content with what you have, because God has said, "Never will I leave you; never will I forsake you." (Heb. 13:5 NIV)

I don't say this out of need, for I have learned to be content in whatever circumstances I am. I know both how to have a little, and I know how to have a lot. In any and all circumstances I have learned the secret of being content—whether well-fed or hungry, whether in abundance or in need. I am able to do all things through Him who strengthens me. (Phil. 4:11–13)

The writer of Hebrews answers the question, "How much is enough?" The answer is, "Be content with what you have." Enough is whatever I have right now. The resources currently at my disposal are enough. I don't need more to answer any longing or need of my heart. I can be content with what I have because of the truth that God is with me, at all times. His presence, not more resources, settles anxiety, insecurity, and dissatisfaction.

In part of his letter to the Philippians, Paul gives more color to the contentment perspective. His experience in life had involved both plenty and lack, both self-sufficiency and dependency. Paul learned contentment as he experienced the indwelling power of "Him who strengthens me." Interestingly, Paul applies contentment to BOTH need and abundance. We tend to think more contentment is needed when we are struggling to live with less than what seems ideal to us. However, Paul's teaching lets us know that when we experience abundance (an American reality) we also deeply need to practice contentment through the strength of Jesus so that we don't fall into its unique traps. Learning to be content is for everyone—not just for those who experience lack!

We've all seen T-shirts with "I can do all things through Christ who strengthens me" on the back—applying the verse to any number of challenges (sports teams, service teams, fighting illness, and more)!

> God's presence, not more resources, settles anxiety, insecurity, and dissatisfaction.

However, in context, this wonderfully famous line from Scripture actually applies to learning contentment. We can learn it because we can do it through the power of Christ's strength. His sufficient grace lets us learn to rest in what we currently have as "enough." He empowers us to practice contentment, even in the face of cultural messages promoting the opposite.

The Key Shift: *A discontentment perspective seeks answers to heart questions in material solutions, expecting that more of something external will solve internal struggles. A contentment perspective recognizes that what I have right now is enough and that God's presence and power answers my heart struggles, fueling my ability to be satisfied with my current circumstances.*

Let's make peace with our financial situation and recognize that more money or less money is never the solution to our heart questions.

Wisdom: Taking Solomon with You to the Mall

Earthly wisdom and heavenly wisdom stand in stark contrast to one another, and you can tell the difference by their fruit. James 3:16–17 says, "For where envy and selfish ambition exist, there is disorder and every kind of evil. But the wisdom from above is first pure, then peace-loving, gentle, compliant, full of mercy and good fruits, without favoritism and hypocrisy."

As a financial advisor to many people through the years, I am familiar with the telltale hallmarks of an earthly mind-set—envy, disorder, and selfish ambition. Earthly wisdom doesn't yield peace or confidence. Instead, with an earthly mentality, money stresses people out, stirs people up, and makes people confused. If this is your reality, be encouraged that adopting a wisdom perspective can radically change the fruit in your financial life.

As promised in James, applying biblical wisdom yields a better outcome: peace, mercy, gentleness, and good fruit—even with financial issues. A wisdom mentality is a new way of thinking about our money. I'm not talking about adopting formulas and rules, but rather a new mind-set altogether—rooted in something far more transcendent than opinions, urges, or formulas.

Have you ever thought about God's wisdom being eternal? Proverbs 8:22 says of wisdom, "The LORD made me at the beginning of His creation, before His works of long ago." When we seek God's wisdom, we are actually aligning ourselves with something that existed from the beginning of time. Take a minute and really let that resonate with your spirit. Before any physical laws of nature existed, wisdom was there. Wisdom is an eternal, indisputable force. Applying God's financial wisdom positions us firmly on a bedrock that our Creator laid before time began.

> Wisdom is an eternal, indisputable force. Applying God's financial wisdom positions us firmly on a bedrock that our Creator laid before time began.

In addition to God's wisdom being eternal, it is also available. James 1:5 says, "Now if any of you lacks wisdom, he should ask God, who gives to all generously and without criticizing, and it will be given to him." God's wisdom doesn't emanate from our thinking, processing, ruminating, planning, or understanding. It comes directly from Him, and we can ask Him for it! I cannot tell you the number of client meetings I have walked into and prayed, "Lord, You promised to give me wisdom, and I am asking for it, in this specific situation." Time and time again, God has answered my prayer for wisdom and has given me words to say and advice to offer that was completely outside of my own under-standing or even inclination. How often do you specifically ask God for His wisdom when you need it? I have found that when I ask Him for supernatural wisdom, I am continually amazed at His generous response!

Finally, God's wisdom meets us where we are today. When we ask Him, He offers wisdom that is fitting for the circumstances we face currently. While some good counsel can be applied long term, other times in life, we receive good advice intended for a unique pur-pose in a specific season. Unfortunately, sometimes with said advice, we tend to continue adhering to it long after it has stopped making sense.

Years ago, on one of many trips to Africa, I had a heart-wrenching encounter with my good friend. Randy was a career missionary, the father of a growing family, and was as fully surrendered financially as anyone I had seen. In fact, his missionary-salary giving was based on a radical challenge that he heard years before in a sermon. The pastor had challenged his audience to consider increasing their giving by 1 percent per year. At the time, my friend was tithing 10 percent. He and his wife considered the challenge and committed to increase their giving by 1 percent. When he and I were talking, his giving was in the 30 percent per year range and he was feeling very pinched financially. The day we talked, he was looking for advice. Due to his commitment made long ago when his finances looked very different, he was feeling overwhelmed and guilty for not being able to find a way "out" without breaking the rule. I encouraged him in the way of grace and to seek God's wisdom about his financial stresses rather than to lean so heavily on a system he had set up for himself so many years prior.

Not all of our financial rules are as altruistic as my friend's, but they often create similar tension for us as we seek to apply them relentlessly, despite changing circumstances or relationships.

In fact, as I've counseled many couples about their finances over the years, much of the tension that I have seen has come from one or both of them having hard-core "formulas" about how they think they should deploy their money. I've met savers, spenders, givers, debt-payers, and tax avoiders . . . all of whom are in conflict with their spouse because they have elevated a "should" about the use of their money to the primary place, without taking into account the whole picture.

The power of wisdom is that it is holistic—it is applied uniquely in different situations and as our circumstances change. Walking in wisdom invites us further into a relationship with the Lord. Walking in wisdom means seeing the big picture, listening to God's truth daily, and applying His principles uniquely to financial circumstances.

The Key Shift: *Wisdom is eternal, supernatural, and available. When we rely on God's wisdom rather than an earthly mind-set, we experience the good fruits mentioned in James 3:16–17.*

Faith: "What Would You Have Me to Do?"

John, a retired cardiac surgeon, was on the front lines of open-heart surgery technology in the 1970s and 1980s. His career was both high risk and high reward. He is no stranger to living boldly, and he was very familiar with making life-altering decisions. Nevertheless, just as his career was beginning to be more and more financially lucrative, he was uncertain about a move his family was planning to make. During this time, we had a powerful conversation that shaped both of our lives.

He and his wife had just built their dream home—an expensive house on a beautiful piece of property—a large tract of land with rolling hills; it was an oasis of calm in the middle of a growing city. John's faith was growing by leaps and bounds, and he came to me with the very earnest question, "Ron, is it okay with God for me to move into my new, large home?"

At the time, I had recently been called into ministry, choosing to walk away from a career that afforded me many nice things. This calling into ministry led my wife and me to downsize our life. It was tempting to apply my experience of downsizing to my friend's similar questions about his home and lifestyle. I believe the Holy Spirit stopped me from falling into that trap. Instead, God gave me wisdom when I turned back to my friend and said, "John, I am not the one to answer that question for you. Have you asked God that question? What would God have you to do?"

My friend spent the next several weeks asking God his question and wrestling with it during his prayer and devotion time. John heard God inviting him to use his home as a place of ministry in his city. Over the next decades in that home, there were countless outreaches, dinners, meetings, and youth events. Many, many people met Jesus in my friend's home—not because it was big, but because he had surrendered his home to God and followed God's direction for its use.

Rather than being afraid of life's struggles, and rather than filling the question-gaps that we all have with other people's opinions, the Bible teaches us about journeying by faith:

Now faith is the reality of what is hoped for, the proof of what is not seen. (Heb. 11:1)

Now without faith it is impossible to please God, for the one who draws near to Him must believe that He exists and rewards those who seek Him. (Heb. 11:6)

Faith bridges the gap between what is reality now and what we hope for. Faith pleases God as it closes the gap between Him and us. Faith stretches us to continue to believe in and rely on God's goodness.

Even though my friend was a man of extreme competence and confidence

> Faith stretches us to continue to believe in and rely on God's goodness.

in his career, his faith journey regarding his home led him to a new habit of placing his ultimate confidence in God and his ultimate dependence on God's direction.

Romans 14:23 states that whatever is not of faith is sin, and Romans 14:5 reminds us that when we take action in our spiritual life, we should be fully convinced in our own minds that what we are doing is good before the Lord. We can see that God wants us to be men and women of faith who act boldly when He leads us, wherever He leads us.

Your financial journey is unique. Beginning to walk in faith before God in your financial life will open you up to new, deeper ways to grow in your walk with Him. Begin to ask God, "What would You have me to do?" and I'll guarantee that you'll be rewarded with a profound richness in your relationship with Him.

The Key Shift: *Jesus was clear in telling us that the world is a place of trouble—this includes financial trouble. A "here and now" perspective limits our view of God and narrows our vision. A faith perspective leads us to deepen our belief in God's character, expanding our relationship with Him as we allow Him to lead us into unknown places of greater impact.*

Important Money Perspectives

You are a steward, managing God's resources.
You can learn to be content with what you have.
You have ready access to eternal, supernatural wisdom.
Your financial life is fertile soil for a powerful faith journey.

Armed with these perspectives, let's set aside our grasshopper mentalities and boldly fight in the land that God has given us to conquer.

Takeaway

After considering contentment, wisdom, and faith perspectives, do you find that one allows you to face your impending battle from a more confident place? How can you begin to reframe your perspective about your financial challenges? Is there a practical way that you can begin to walk in contentment, wisdom, or faith regarding your money?

God desires for you to experience peace and contentment in His plan for you and your finances. The only way to know His plan is to begin asking Him and listening to Him. Psalm 46:10 says, "Be still, and know that I am God" (NIV). When we listen to His voice, we are reminded of His care, provision, and power in our lives. We are reminded that He is God and He knows the next step.

A Perspective on Success, Security, and Significance

We all know the saying "money doesn't buy happiness," but most of us still believe deep down that some shift in our financial circumstances will finally make us feel **successful**, **secure**, or **significant**. In my years of experience, I've seen that people at all income levels pursue financial answers to solve these heart issues. One day I discovered that even the wealthiest people in the world struggle in this arena!

In the 1990s, Dave and I served on a board of directors together and lived in the same city. Dave owned an airplane, so I had the privilege of riding on his plane a few times a year as we traveled to board meetings. Hanging out with him opened doors to more luxury than I'd ever dreamed of experiencing. One time, he and his wife even took Judy and me on a vacation to a private, tropical island. Suffice it to say that I've never experienced anything like it since!

When I would travel with Dave and sit on his plane, thoughts such as *Who could wish for more than this?* would run through my head while knowing full well that money doesn't buy happiness. Still, it was difficult for me to imagine how my friend could feel anything but successful, secure, and significant all the time.

On one of our trips, Dave told me that he was getting ready to meet with the sultan of Brunei who was, at that time, the world's wealthiest man. Brunei is a sovereign state on the island of Borneo, that has one of the highest ratios of gross domestic product per capita due to its extensive oil and natural gas resources. A little known, very wealthy country with the world's richest man at the helm.

I leaned forward in my seat, interested to hear what THAT meeting would look like!

To my great surprise, I learned that the meeting would take place on the sultan's compound, but by video. Dave would be ushered into a special room where he would interact with the sultan via closed circuit television. Although my friend was recognized globally as an upstanding businessman, possessing fastidious integrity, there was absolutely no chance the sultan would meet with him in person. In fact, the sultan met with no one in person. The world's wealthiest man trusted no one to be in the same room with him.

Pondering this reality, I asked myself the question, *How much money does it take to be **secure**?* Apparently, there is never enough—even for the wealthiest man on earth.

As our conversation continued, Dave said, "You know, Ron, it's easy to be intimidated by that level of wealth." *WHAT!?* I thought. I found it tough to fathom my affluent friend would be intimidated by any level of wealth—once you had enough to buy airplanes and islands, didn't that solve the heart issues of feeling **successful** and **significant**? Apparently not. Not even islands and airplanes will do it.

This interaction illustrates the truth that I've been discovering and sharing for years: You (or me, or the airplane guy, or the sultan of an oil-rich empire) can never accumulate enough to feel secure, successful, or significant. We just can't, because money will never be the answer to these heart issues.

So guess what? Money really doesn't buy happiness!

4

Five Wise Principles

Have you ever been in totally over your head?

I have.

I had been invited to testify in front of a congressional subcommittee. If you've ever been flipping the channels and found yourself watching a riveting live feed on C-SPAN, you can probably picture the heavily paneled room, the bank of microphones, the senators all looking down from tiered seating at the front of the room, and the daunted-looking testifiers answering important people's questions.

I was the daunted guy.

The question on the table, from Senator Dodd of Connecticut, was, "What advice about money would you give the American family?"

I swallowed hard, knowing my answer was going to sound really, really simple to him.

"Well, Senator, I would tell them four things. Spend less than they earn, avoid debt, save for the unexpected, and set long-term goals."

The senator picked up his pencil and asked me to repeat myself.

I did.

Then he looked down at me over his glasses and said, "It seems that would work at any income level."

(By now, I was gaining my footing and decided to take my chances. . . .)

"Yes, sir. Even for the United States government."

And there you have it—the day I was in over my head and gave a United States Senator advice on how to run the economy. Gulp.

Key #2: Five Wise Principles

Twenty-five years later I am still confident that the advice I gave works. These four principles, along with the biblical principle of giving generously, are rooted in the timeless wisdom from God's Word and, accordingly, are timeless, transcendent, and true. God's Word is always right, always relevant, and will never change. This is true for my finances, your finances, and the finances being worked out at a macroeconomic, government level, as well.

---

5 Wise Principles

1. Spend less than you earn
2. Avoid debt
3. Give generously
4. Save for the unexpected
5. Set long-term goals

On that day in Washington, D.C., I realized with fresh clarity that these simple principles had always worked and would continue to work for every person, class, company, or government.

Wisdom is powerful. God is gracious to give us much wisdom in His Word. He is especially gracious to give us abundant, clear wisdom about money—one of the hardest topics in this mortal life.

When we follow wise principles, we gain an unshakable confidence that we are aligned with truth, no matter the outcome.

> When we follow wise principles, we gain an unshakable confidence.

No Matter the Outcome

I'd like to take a turn toward realism here. Sometimes, simple wisdom can strike us as being, well, simple. Perhaps pie in the sky or not informed. So let's talk for a minute about the realistic nature of being human in a human economic system.

You may be thinking through multiple scenarios as you consider the wise principles. Maybe you're thinking, *What about the recent economic downturn? What if we end up engaged in another war or terrorism erupts at home? What if oil prices fall (or rise) and the stock market loses its footing? What if something unexpected happens to my family? Will those wise principles still really make sense and work?*

There's a reality that is very obvious but often overlooked and, therefore, usually missed: economic uncertainty is certain.

When I was born in 1942, America was at war with Hitler, Stalin, Mussolini, and Hirohito. The economy was growing due to the war industry, but the future was very uncertain. Fear was rampant.

While still a young man living in my parents' home, the Cold War took hold and I spent many days at school hiding under my desk, practicing for when a nuclear bomb would fall. I was afraid.

During my years as a college student, the country went through a recession and we began to endure the long, drawn-out journey through the Vietnam War. In contrast, the emergency posed by the Cuban Missile Crisis was frighteningly riveting. Americans were uncertain.

Throughout my early thirties, we experienced great economic uncertainty as the oil embargo, Watergate, and the decision to go off of the gold standard all made men like me wonder what the future would hold for our children. One of the most popular books at the time was *The Late Great Planet Earth*, a book predicting the end of the world in 1976. It sold millions of copies. Corruption and doomsday predictions were prevalent, and fear was the lead story.

When I was in my early forties and had been counseling clients from a biblical perspective for several years, the economy was like a roller coaster. I had to talk my clients through a prime rate of 21 percent, mortgage rates of 14 percent and gold selling at $800 an ounce. An inflation mind-set was the order of the day, and my clients became very anxious—our phones rang off the hook.

In my fifties, we experienced a war in Iraq, an out-of-control deficit, a recession, and more political scandals. Our economic footing seemed pretty uncertain.

In my early sixties, we experienced terror on our soil on 9/11 and then saw the technology bubble burst and Wall Street corruption exposed. No one was immune; we knew danger was imminent.

Today, I'm in my mid-seventies. You can read the paper today and tell me if it is any different. I can guarantee you that there are headlines this very day about societal fear, political uncertainty, economic upset, or corporate corruption.

Each new decade will inevitably bring new threats, new fears, new upheavals, and new ways that the economy can go awry. This reality is just a reflection of Jesus' statement in John 16:33, "You will have suffering in this world." Jesus goes on to say, "Be courageous! I have conquered the world." Biblical financial wisdom gives us courage in the face of inevitable financial uncertainty.

Back to Stewardship

So, we have two sides of this coin: wisdom is transcendent and timeless; economic uncertainty is certain.

In the downturn of 2008, a financial advisor friend lost more than half of his retirement in the stock market. Meanwhile, he was fielding calls at work from other advisors whom he led, encouraging them to stay the course of wisdom and not give into wild schemes derived from panic. But in his heart, he was uncertain and fearful, too. One night after work, my friend sat with his wife and took a hard look at their recent losses and the implications of those losses on their future and their lifestyle. It was a sobering journey into uncertainty for them. Before long, he began leading them back through these five wise money management principles out loud . . .

"Did we spend less than we made?" (yes)

"Have we avoided debt?" (yes)

"Have we saved money along the way?" (yes)

"Do we give generously?" (yes)

"Have we had financial goals that have guided our decisions?"
(yes)

After seeing their "yes" answers to all five of these questions, my friend and his wife gained a sense of peace. They could rest knowing that they had followed a path of financial wisdom, positioning them most effectively to deal with the crazy economic downturn they were experiencing. As the sovereign owner of their resources, God could be trusted. God was in charge of both the size of their portfolio and the turns of the market.

Trusting the Lord's sovereignty while sitting confidently in our ability to steward resources wisely is something totally unique. Let's take a deeper look at the *Five Wise Principles*—the things we **can** do in our financial lives to exercise wise stewardship—and consider why they are so powerful.

1. Spend less than you earn because every success in your financial life depends on this habit.

When God made Adam and Eve, He gave them meaningful work to do. Tending the garden and naming the animals—forms of physical, mental, and creative work—existed even in paradise, before sin entered the picture. Genesis 2:15 says, "The LORD God took the man and placed him in the garden of Eden to work it and watch over it." Work is part of God's original design for man. As such, work has rewards.

Work brings dignity.

Work allows us to express our talents.

Work creates progress.

Work contributes to a functioning community.

Work yields income.

When we work, we receive the "fruit" of our labor in the form of a paycheck. I believe that we rob work itself of some of work's inherent value when we fail to respect the boundaries of our paychecks and start to live beyond our means. Scripture teaches very clearly that our work and our long-term wealth or savings are intimately connected.

A few of my favorite Scriptures that relate to this principle are these:

Idle hands make one poor, but diligent hands bring riches. (Prov. 10:4)

Wealth gained hastily will dwindle, but whoever gathers little by little will increase it. (Prov. 13:11 ESV)

God has also given riches and wealth to every man, and He
has allowed him to enjoy them, take his reward, and rejoice
in his labor. This is a gift of God. (Eccl. 5:19)

Ultimately, if we do not live within our means, we will not
accomplish our desires and plans in other areas of our financial life.
These verses encourage us toward steady and consistent pursuit to
spend less than we make over time. The result is increase and abundance. If we do not spend less money
than we bring in, it is impossible to
achieve any financial goals and to move
into any of the other principles. Without
margin (the difference between what
comes in and what goes out) we cannot
avoid debt, give, or accumulate for the
unexpected that will come. And our
goals cannot be met. If we do not follow
this first principle, we will never have
the flexibility or freedom to pursue the
goals and objectives that God gives to

> If we do not live within our means, we will not accomplish our desires and plans in other areas of our financial life.

us. The opposite is also true: Following this first principle will give
the flexibility and freedom to pursue the goals and objectives that
God gives to us.

Often, when facing a tight budget, people immediately seek to
add more income. Perhaps they take a second job. Maybe a spouse
goes back to work. I would love to challenge that "how can I get
more?" thinking and encourage you to make every effort to spend less

than you earn right now, today, before you jump to adding income. (Of course, I am making an assumption that you are employed at the level that makes sense for your training, experience, etc.) Ultimately, it may make sense for you to add income in order to accomplish your goals, but I believe that respecting the paycheck you have and living within it is the first step toward accomplishing any long-term financial desire or goal.

The gift of work is a rich gift, and it is worth it to begin to enjoy the fruit of your labor by living within your means and having financial margin. Opportunities expand when we practice this very wise biblical principle.

2. Avoid debt because debt always mortgages the future.

Yikes. Mortgage. Who wants another one of those?

Have you ever pondered the reality that any debt we have puts a burden on our future? How many of us have ever let some form of a household chore pile up while we were busy with other things . . . perhaps laundry went undone or bills went unpaid for many days, or maybe we just kept cramming stuff into the storage shed out back thinking that someday we would clean it out. We are all familiar with putting off mundane or distasteful chores because of desires in the present moment. "I'll get to it tomorrow." Then, when tomorrow comes, we wonder why we didn't deal with yesterday's stuff yesterday.

Like work, time is also a gift from God, given to us as a blessing. Scripture teaches that His mercies are new every morning and that God oversees the rising and setting of the sun. The gift of time allows us to get things done. It lets us pursue relationships. It provides space for us to rest and heal. It gives us manageable chunks in which to attack big goals like a college degree or running a half marathon. When we rely on debt to ease today's financial load, we are burdening tomorrow's time, robbing it of flexibility and availability.

The car payment I take on today means that tomorrow I will have to earn a certain income.

The student loan I agree to today means that I will have to earn a certain, higher level of income down the road and I may not have flexibility in what job I take after my degree is done.

The clothes I "need" to put on my credit card today to be ready for the vacation I'm taking mean that I will not be able to enjoy dinners out or have freedom to respond to the car repairs next month.

The bigger home that I feel compelled to live in affects my retirement opportunity, delaying it by several years.

Debt always mortgages the future.

The Bible states it very simply in Proverbs 22:7. "The rich rule over the poor, and the borrower is a slave to the lender."

Being in debt puts us in a position of servitude. It mortgages our tomorrow and it means that we have an obligation to serve the lender first—before we save our money or give it or choose to spend it on family memories. Debt payments demand first priority, no matter what. Scripture goes so far as to make debt repayment a moral issue. Psalm 37:21 says, "The wicked man borrows and does not repay, but the righteous one is gracious and giving." Both paying debts back and being "gracious and giving" are upright practices in the eyes of the Lord, but I would speak from experience in saying that being a gracious giver is a lot more fulfilling than being a faithful debt repayer!

3. Give generously because giving breaks the power of money.

I can't explain it, but I've seen it over and over in my own life and in the lives of clients I have counseled. There is a freedom in giving money away that exists nowhere else in a person's financial experience.

My favorite analogy for this freedom is the image of an open hand. When I hold my hand open, with my financial resources available to God at all times for His purposes, I experience freedom. I know that He can take away from my hand and that He can add to my hand, but something about the process of giving provides freedom to trust Him more fully.

Jesus used the analogy of treasure when He taught about giving. He said,

> "Don't collect for yourselves treasures on earth, where moth and rust destroy and where thieves break in and steal. But collect for yourselves treasures in heaven, where neither moth nor rust destroys, and where thieves don't break in and steal. For where your treasure is, there your heart will be also." (Matt. 6:19–21)

Jesus had the distinct advantage of knowing firsthand the difference between Earth and eternity. He witnessed the entropy and decay on planet Earth and knew the contrasting glory and longevity of heaven. He urged His followers to lay up heavenly treasures by putting their financial resources into eternal accounts. In the process, He knew that their hearts would then become captivated and motivated by eternal purposes. The "treasure principle" says that our hearts and our money are inextricably linked—our hearts always follow our money.

If our hearts follow our money, then we can break the power that money holds over our hearts by giving it away. Giving sends a powerful message that we believe in God's goodness, we trust God's ownership, and we are about God's agenda. And, when we give, we deeply experience the reality of His goodness, His ownership, and His agenda in our lives.

There's really nothing like it. I hope you will trust me when I tell you that power of financial generosity is radical to transform entire lives. If you have not experienced it firsthand, I'm eager for you to have the privilege!

4. Plan for financial margin because the unexpected will occur.

The last two wise financial principles are tied very strongly to the first one: "spend less than you earn." They work together like dominoes.

If I spend less than I earn, I will have flexibility and I can decide what to do with the extra.

Then, if I decide to use some of the extra to build margin into my finances, I will be able to effectively deal with unexpected expenses.

And, even better, I can then begin to save the extra for long-term financial goals, allowing me to pursue God-given desires and priorities in my future.

Many of us get caught in financial binds because we have not planned for short-term margin—we haven't addressed our need to have savings in the bank to cushion against the unexpected. Maybe we budget our money so that we can save, but often that money goes straight toward retirement or college funds that are inaccessible to us in the short term, leaving us high and dry when "stuff" happens.

Jesus said, "You will have suffering in this world" (John 16:33). Suffering, including financial suffering, is part and parcel to being human. Accordingly, we must prepare for the unexpected by having short-term, emergency savings and by having long-term, goal-focused savings. Solomon talked about the ant, reminding us that, "Without leader, administrator, or ruler, it prepares its provisions in summer; it gathers its food during harvest" (Prov. 6:7–8). Jesus talked about planning for the future and counting the cost when He said, "For which of you, wanting to build a tower, doesn't first sit down and calculate the cost to see if he has enough to complete it?" (Luke 14:28).

Financial wisdom says that we need to have accessible savings, allowing us to deal with short-term trouble and helping us grow toward long-term goals.

5. Set long-term goals because there is always a trade-off between the short term and the long term.

This is the fun part! My kids like to give me a hard time for having them set goals every year as a part of their birthday celebration when they were growing up. Even though they moaned and groaned, they always enjoyed looking back to the last year's goals to see what had been accomplished and to remember what continued to be important to them. Written goals are powerful motivators, and research proves it.[5]

Finances always involve a trade-off between the short term and the long term. If we don't have long-term goals, we simply won't know how to prioritize our spending and saving in the short term. Because money is a tool to accomplish other goals and objectives, setting goals gives us clarity about how to use our "tool"—money—toward our savings, debt repayment, budgeting, or giving.

Also, having written goals means that we are far more likely to continue to be financially disciplined and to create good financial habits. Habits take hold because we have a strong "why" motivating our habits. Goals provide the why—the necessary motivation. In some ways, written goals close the loop with all of the other wise financial habits. Knowing why we are doing something via a written goal helps us to have a starting point, it helps us to stay the course, and it lets us know when we are done and can look to other, new goals.

Goals tie our habits to our hearts.

Proverbs 29:18 (NASB) says, "Where there is no vision, the people are unrestrained." Writing goals is a way that we clarify the vision that God has given us for our lives. Pursuing them provides us with a pathway and helps us to make more confident decisions today.

> **Goals tie our habits to our hearts.**

And, better still, as followers of Christ, we are privileged to be able to set goals with God's input and vision. Ephesians 2:10, one of my favorite verses, says, "For we are His creation, created in Christ Jesus for good works, which God prepared ahead of time so that we should walk in them." God has prepared works for us to do already. When we ask Him to speak into our goals, He can move us into those works and allow us the privilege of completing them.

Last House Standing

A few years ago, I saw a remarkable depiction of the parable that Jesus told in Matthew 7:24–28, where He taught His disciples about the power of a firm foundation. In the parable, He challenged His audience to act on the words they had heard—to put into practice His teaching. In doing so, they would have a house built on the rock, able to stand, rather than a flimsy house on a sandy foundation.

After Hurricane Ike ravaged Galveston Island, there was one house standing on the Gulf Coast side of Gilchrist, Texas. The image of a yellow frame home surrounded by rubble on all sides is striking. The fortunate home belonged to Pam and Warren Adams, who had already been through the horror of Hurricane Rita.

After Rita struck in 2005, the Adamses' home was destroyed. Determined to rebuild and to stay on the island despite the risks, the Adamses hired local experts to build their home with extensive hurricane protection. Their new house had fourteen-foot columns, putting them at twenty-two feet above sea level. After Hurricane Ike rolled through, they were one of very few salvageable homes that remained.[6]

So how is this story related to our discussion about money?

First is the obvious tie to Jesus' parable of a firm foundation. The Adamses' home had a foundation that allowed it to stand in the face of a giant storm surge. When we follow the five biblically wise financial principles, we are building our "house" to stand against the storms that life brings. We are doing all we can do as wise stewards.

The second lesson I see is the same one my financial planner friend learned after the recent economic downturn. The Adamses had to move out of their home while the damage was repaired. Even though it stood, it was damaged in the storm. Following wise principles doesn't guarantee a life free of financial upset or trouble. But it does mean we will be in the best shape possible to face the storms of life.

Financial success is not an elusive goal. While there may not ever be a pot at the end of the rainbow or a money tree growing in the backyard, and while you may not suddenly inherit a million dollars from an unknown aunt, you absolutely can take the bull by the horns and apply the five biblical financial principles to your life with complete confidence that they will yield the fruit of peace and confidence in your financial life.

I'll take that promise all the way to the United States Senate.

Takeaway

Awareness opens the door to transformative change. Now you are better equipped to understand your own financial reality and able to alter the trajectory of your financial life by putting these Five Wise Principles into practice:

1. Spend less than you earn because every success in your financial life depends on this habit.
2. Avoid debt because debt always mortgages the future.
3. Give generously because giving breaks the power of money.
4. Plan for financial margin because the unexpected will occur.
5. Set long-term goals because there is always a trade-off between the short term and the long term.

How can you begin to integrate one principle in your life today? Don't worry about making it a huge thing, but take at least one small step toward implementing what you have learned.

5

Only One Pie

When our kids were young, we used to regularly host missionaries in our home on their way to and from the mission field. Most of our missionary friends anticipated supplies they would need months and even years in advance and would shop while on these trips home. Judy graciously hosted them by taking them to the local A&P and Kmart stores—the 1970s answers to Costco and Amazon Prime.

I remember coming home from work one day after Judy had spent the day shopping for supplies with a missionary friend. As we closed the door on our bedroom that night, Judy couldn't wait to share their experience. "It was remarkable! We turned the corner on the cereal aisle and she just stopped cold. She couldn't move for a solid two minutes while she looked at the variety of options on the shelves." The woman had been used to one, maybe two, options for dry cereal for the past few years in Africa. The overwhelming nature of the cereal aisle left her speechless . . . partly in wonder, partly in distress.

As we processed the day together, I had an "aha" moment, seeing the complexity of our culture from our friend's perspective. Even now

I remember this incident and the complexity we navigate when I walk down the cereal aisle. Our daily lives are complicated and growing more so. I am assaulted by complexity when I go with my grandson to his favorite video game store. As I look around, I wonder how he can even begin to know which game is fun, or good, or right for his age, or . . . anything. The options are endless, and I would rather just turn around and walk out!

Financial decisions can be a bit like visiting the cereal aisle or the video game store. When I open my online banking center, I see the transactions float across the screen like a never-ending series of either-or, if-then, because-why decisions I have faced over the last two weeks.

- Should we eat in or out tonight? Is my time or my money more valuable after a long day of work?
- If my daughter joins the lacrosse team, then she will need equipment. Can we pay for that, too?
- Because I signed up for auto-renew on my account, the $79.95 hit me right between the eyes. Why did I do that!?

Every transaction in my account represents choices I've made trying to sort through the static of options, but I can be left feeling that my money has morphed into a living being and is eating its way through my best intentions. Saving for vacation? (CHOMP— *Maybe next month*) Paying off more credit card balance this month? (CHOMP—*I guess lacrosse is worth it for her.*) Going on a date with my wife this weekend? (CHOMP—*That eating out thing we did after we both got home late last Tuesday must have been our date. I wish I'd known!)* It seems I've fed the money beast to my own detriment. *(But there's always next month!)*

If money were as simple as choosing between Cheerios versus Raisin Bran or a fight game versus a racing game, I'd be in great shape. The problem is, deciding what to do with my money feels more like shopping the cereal aisle at the Super Walmart or searching Google for good books. Endless options, limited resources!

Two Fancy Definitions

Now that you and I are suitably depressed over this predicament, I'd like to define our problem by giving it a fancy name that I've used in my financial advising over the years. I call this predicament having "simultaneous competing priorities."

Just to break it down:

Simultaneous: happening all at once
Competing: fighting (and loudly)
Priorities: about options that I really, genuinely think are important

You can see the problem—important stuff fighting for attention all at the same time. Really, I bet that you can FEEL the problem.

Because we have these simultaneous competing priorities, we also face confusing financial decisions.

And so, while we are tuned into this problem, let's just go ahead and make it worse. My fancy definition for "financial decision making" has always been "the allocation of limited resources among unlimited alternatives."

Just to break it down (again):

Allocation: choosing how to spend
Limited: not quite enough
Resources: of my hard-earned money
Unlimited: on neverending, all that is "Google-able"
Alternatives: stuff, makes, models, causes, dreams, plans, upgrades, etc.

In short, we want our money to do everything for us that we can envision it doing, but none of us has enough money to make that "everything" dream a reality. We have limited resources. We have unlimited alternatives. We make hard choices by allocating our money toward some alternatives instead of others. Financial decisions always involve this type of choice.

The combination of having "simultaneous competing priorities" and knowing that my financial decisions are the process of "allocating limited resources among unlimited alternatives" causes me to sit up a bit straighter in my chair and say, "Eureka! This explains my angst!!" This reality is the reason why I fuss and strain over the reality on the online banking screen. This reality is why I wriggle internally when I hear something on the radio that makes me think I ought to be saving, planning, spending, or giving differently. This reality is why I fight with my wife about financial things that seem awfully petty, even in the moment. This reality is why I can't ever seem to get it "right" when it comes to money.

I prioritize savings and grow frustrated with acting stingy and boring all the time.

I prioritize debt repayment and worry that I am depriving my family of memories and fun.

I prioritize making memories with my family and realize that my credit card balance ballooned and my intentions to give to my friend's charity just won't happen this month.

I squeeze one area of my financial life and another area spontaneously balloons.

There are no independent financial decisions. We can spend money any way that we want, but we can only spend it once.

Key #3: The Pie

Let me propose something transformational: Money Is a Circle, Not a Line.

In our world, we think of money as being linear when we hear about "plans" (savings, debt repayment, spending, etc.) and "budgets." We know that money has numbers in it, and most of our experience with numbers involves hard and fast equations and rules. We mistakenly believe that we can tie money down, box it in, plan it out, and then wipe our dirty hands clean of it and get on with our "real" life.

Money is not a line. We don't make one decision and then move on from that decision, leaving it permanently behind. Money is a circle. Financial decisions in one area impact our financial realities in other areas, sometimes leading us to visit certain decisions more than once as circumstances change. I find it helpful to think of money as a pie, in fact.

My money chases its tail, but it does that because that is its nature. My spending decisions are not designed to be distinct from my savings decisions. My giving decisions are not designed to be separate from my debt decisions. They go together and must inhabit the same circle, the same "pie."

When I understand that my money is an interconnected circle, the goal of my financial life moves from checking off items in a list to becoming an adept balancer of spinning plates inside of the circus ring called money.

Money and life are inextricably linked. While this reality is sometimes frustrating, I would like to set you free to accept this reality.

We cannot straighten out the circle. We cannot unbend the arc that bends financial choices back onto other financial choices.

We can, however, learn to live contentedly inside of the circle, once we understand both its component parts and the guiding biblical wisdom that informs each of these parts.

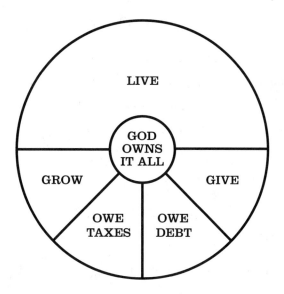

LIVE: Spend less than you earn, because every financial success depends on this habit.

GIVE: Giving breaks the power of money.

OWE DEBT: Debt always mortgages the future.

OWE TAXES: Pay taxes with gratitude, because taxes are symptomatic of God's provision.

GROW: Set long-term goals, because there is always a trade-off between the short term and long term.

So, step one is to recognize that the knot we are trying to untie and lie flat is really a circle. It will never be a line.

Step two is to simplify our understanding of what lies inside of the circle in order to learn to balance our competing priorities and allocate our limited resources with more confidence and clarity.

Only One Pie

For years, I've taught that there are only five things anyone can do with money: save it, pay off debt, give it, pay taxes, or spend it on lifestyle. A few years ago, my good friend Mitch Anthony came up with a handy way to label the five uses of money:

LIVE: the money I *live* on
GIVE: the money I *give* away
OWE: the money I pay for *debt* and *taxes*
GROW: the money I *save*

I shared Mitch's "live, give, owe, grow" rhyme with my wife, Judy. She loved it. She could easily remember it and the five uses I'd been teaching for years suddenly crystallized in her mind. Since then, I've been using the pie diagram with "live, give, owe, grow" to teach financial decision making.

Reducing financial options down to five fundamental things that we can do with money simplifies our spending decisions. When we understand that there are only five pieces of the pie and every decision fits into one of those pieces, it simplifies our thinking. When we know that money can only go into one of the five wedges, we have more clarity to sort through priorities and make confident decisions.

As we come to understand the pie and how it simplifies financial thinking, remember that there is only one pie in each of our lives. The pie may be big or it may be small, but none of us have an "all you can eat" pie! Our individual pie represents all of the money we have to work with at any given time—no more and no less.

Before online banking and the virtual disappearance of the paper check register, I had a client who added "deposits" to her register ($500, $1,000, $2,000 at a time) whenever the recorded balance threatened to fall below $0. The problem: she never actually deposited any real money into the bank. Writing money into the check register was her way of pretending there was more pie available than was reality. Her habit also became a source of great financial stress!

> There is only one pie in each of our lives.

Most of us don't blatantly treat our money like it grows on trees, but many of us do mental gymnastics to try to stretch the boundaries of the pie when they are, in fact, not elastic. Ignoring low balance alerts from the bank, putting "extras" on the credit card, and intending to save but never actually doing so are all ways of tricking ourselves into thinking the boundaries of the pie aren't real.

As I already said, it's important to make peace with the limits of your pie—your financial reality—before you go trying to add more money to the mix with extra incomes or quick fixes. Being content with what you have is

> Being content with what you have is the starting point for sorting out your "simultaneous competing priorities."

the starting point for sorting out your "simultaneous competing priorities."

The Power of the Pie

I have avoided using the "B" word as much as possible. As soon as I say it—"budget"—many of you will run for the hills (or close the book and take the dog for a walk or empty the dishwasher).

In my experience, using the pie diagram provides a viable alternative to deep-dive budgeting for all personality types. For those of you who just cannot stand the thought of attaching line items to your fun and for others who live and breathe spreadsheets, the pie diagram is a great way to get a big-picture view of how your budget matches up with your priorities. Tackling a budget by way of the pie diagram makes the process less overwhelming. It is easier to wrap your mind around each of the five pieces than to take a line-item look at all of the detail that makes up those pieces. You may ultimately decide to go deep into one or more of the wedges, but the process I'm going to show you is a great starting point!

Looking at last year's finances, let's see how the pie diagram simplifies our understanding of where our money is going and reveals whether our spending reflects our stated priorities. (I bet you can do it in under a half an hour. It can be done easily, with the possible exception of unearthing the documents!) Here's how it works:

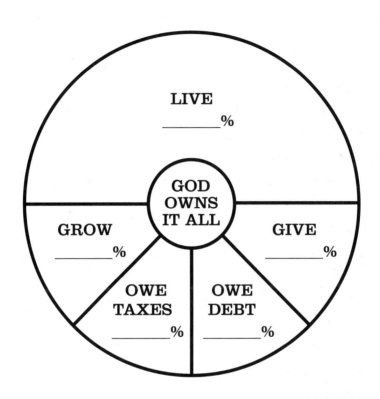

1. Find last year's tax return; use it for the next three steps.

2. Record last year's total income: $_____

3. Record how much you gave: $_____
   - Your giving as a percentage of income: _____%

4. Record how much you paid in taxes: $_____
   - Your taxes as a percentage of income: _____%

5. Find your debt statements from last year.

6. Add up the payments (car, student) and the interest (credit card).

    ** Record how much you paid: $_____

    • Your debt payments as a percentage of income: _____%

7. Find records of last year's savings.

8. Add them up, and record how much you saved: _____

    • Your savings as a percentage of income: _____%

9. Add 3, 4, 6, and 8, below:

    (3) Spent on Give $_____

    (4) Spent on Owe Taxes $_____

    (6) Spent on Owe Debt $_____

    (8) Spent on Grow $_____

    Total: $_____

10. Find your Live amount by subtracting your total from last year's income.

    Last Year's Income $_____

    Minus Total from #9: $_____

    Last Year's Live Amount $_____

    Your Live amount as a percentage of income _____%

** In general, it's best to count "Debt" as scheduled debt that I pay on a regular basis such as minimum credit card payments, student debt, car debt, etc. I consider credit card bills paid off in full every month not as debt, but as just managing your cash flow in the "Live" wedge, and I consider mortgage debt to be a part of the "Live" wedge. These are not hard and fast rules, but ways of sorting out the difference between some of the potentially blurry line between "Live" and "Owe." If you'd rather only count interest in your "Owe" category, that would be another approach. Or, if you'd rather count your entire payment for your mortgage, that also works. Please apply your personal convictions as you sort out your numbers.

Now you have everything you need to write the appropriate numbers and percentages into the appropriate wedges of your pie. When you do, you probably see your money in a new light. The power of the pie diagram exercise is that it reveals whether or not your priorities are aligned with your actual spending.

Because of simultaneous competing priorities, and because of the fact that some priorities yell really loudly due to culture or kids or life demands or the unexpected, sometimes our real-life pie looks very different. Deep down we may wish for a different pie. The truth is that you can start today with your current pie and now make decisions in light of this new knowledge.

The pie diagram helps us to see that there are no independent financial decisions. Spending money in one area always means that we are choosing NOT to spend money in another area. Vacation over car fund savings. Debt repayment over date night. College fund over giving more. All of our financial decisions are integrated.

The pie diagram shows us that the longer term our perspective, the better our decision today. When we take a long view, with long-term priorities in mind, we are able to make wiser, more informed financial decisions in the face of simultaneous competing priorities.

And the pie diagram reveals that financial maturity is being able to give up today's desires for future benefits. Those of us who are parents know what it means to celebrate when our children begin to exercise delayed gratification. I believe that it is also cause for celebration when we, as adults, exercise financial maturity by delaying today's urges to meet tomorrow's needs!

Once we understand what our pie looks like, we can start with the reality of today's situation and begin to shift our decisions so that next year's pie reflects our true priorities more closely. Year after year. Eventually closing the gap between our goals and our reality.

The Way It Usually Works

If your pie doesn't match your priorities, take heart! The dissonance between financial priorities and financial realities is symptomatic of real-world pressure.

In my observation, most people prioritize the wedges of the pie this way:

1. **Live.** We have to live. We have to pay rent, feed our kids, and board the dog when we go on vacation. Among a million other things.
2. **Owe.** We also have to pay debts and taxes. If we don't, creditors will come looking for us. So we pay them.
3. **Grow.** We want to save for the future. When we have margin, most of us respond by putting money away for something important that comes later.
4. **Give.** We want to give. When we feel moved by a need or have the financial margin on a Sunday morning, we really want to give.

This "default" order of priorities puts pressure on what's at the bottom (savings and giving) as what's at the top (living and owing) consumes most of our resources. Money flows down the priority pipeline, and it is progressively less available the further down it goes.

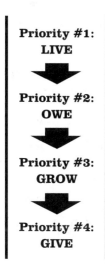

TYPICAL PRIORITY PIPELINE:

Money flows down the priority pipeline. It is progressively less available the further down it goes. Most people prioritize living and owing first, squeezing out growing and giving.

This inadvertent priority order happens when we allow our financial life to happen **to us** rather than taking consistent responsibility for stewarding the wedges of our pie. It's the very real order of events in most people's lives.

The Way It Can Work

In contrast, when we approach our priorities from a biblical perspective, the pressure is applied in a different direction. In Scripture, there are two productive uses of money, two obligatory uses of money, and one consumptive use of money.

1. **Give and Grow.** These two uses of money are *productive*. Giving money yields earthly and eternal fruit, and saving money benefits our future as well.
2. **Owe Debt and Owe Taxes.** These uses are *obligatory*, and it is our moral duty to pay them.
3. **Live.** This use of money is *consumptive*. It is the wedge of the pie that usually takes up the most space. By tending to the other areas first, and intentionally, we can freely enjoy what is left in the live portion without fear or guilt.

If we choose to prioritize our money with this flow of emphasis, we are applying wisdom to our finances. The pressure at the bottom is now on our lifestyle spending, where we wrestle with questions like "How much is enough?" and "How do I practice contentment?"—important questions that make space for our financial lives to be an ongoing dialogue with the Lord in our faith journey. It takes a bold man or woman to begin to live out of a different priority system. I can tell you with complete confidence that the bold men and women I have known have been the most financially confident and content, hands down.

Priority #1:
GIVE

Priority #2:
GROW

Priority #3:
OWE

Priority #4:
LIVE

BIBLICALLY WISE
PRIORITY PIPELINE:

The pressure on the bottom is now on lifestyle spending where we wrestle with important questions that make space for our financial lives to be an ongoing dialogue with the Lord.

Have you ever heard of the "Butterfly Effect"? The Butterfly Effect is a concept that states that small causes can have large effects. The analogy goes something like this: if a butterfly flaps its wings in Asia, that small disturbance of wind will ultimately determine when and how a hurricane forms in the Atlantic Ocean weeks later, an idea that has its origin in chaos theory. The Butterfly Effect is an appropriate analogy for our finances. Small shifts in our priorities have huge effects in the future! What do you want your priority pipeline to look like? Beginning to prioritize our financial decisions differently will, over time, shift our pie so that our spending matches our true priorities.

Takeaway

Take some time to do the pie exercise on pages (75–76). As you consider the current reality of your pie, does it reflect your priorities?

Divide up your pie as you would like it to look in the diagram below:

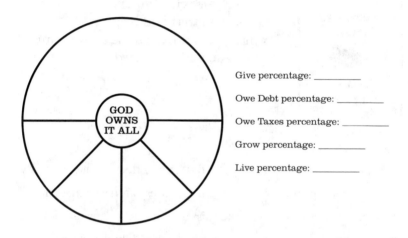

Give percentage: _____

Owe Debt percentage: _____

Owe Taxes percentage: _____

Grow percentage: _____

Live percentage: _____

I'll bet you can identify a change you could make to move your pie to align with your priorities. I challenge you to "go for it" by making that change today, even in the face of those pesky simultaneous competing priorities.

ADAM AND NORA

The Story of a Better Decision

Adam and Nora are deciding whether to move into a bigger home. Their three young children are growing and they would like to live in a home that has a play space for their kids, in a neighborhood where they can be a part of a more tight-knit community. They are careful with their money and have paid down most of their mortgage on their current home, so deciding to move would put them in a position of having significantly more debt, something that brings hesitation. Also, they have different driving motivations. Adam really wants to be debt free and to contribute money to their retirement more aggressively, but he loves the idea of grilling out in the backyard with neighbors and being plugged into a summer swim league, since he was a swimmer in high school. Nora, on the other hand, would love to have the financial margin to send their children to Christian school at some point, but she relishes the thought of having a home where other children feel free to come enjoy a spacious, welcoming environment. There's a new subdivision being built just around the corner from their current home. The new homes have basements and the subdivision is designed to foster community via the swimming pool, the play areas near the bus stop, and the sidewalks. Homes in the neighborhood are considerably more expensive, but they could reasonably afford the mortgage given that Nora recently went back to work as a physical therapist two days a week.

In this case study, how do Adam and Nora make this decision? Because of our simultaneous competing priorities and our limited resources, financial decisions are complicated; they can be very complicated. Over the years, I've relied on a few tried and true decision-making principles that minimize some of the common pitfalls of decision making. I first learned these principles in the 1970s, and they actually come out of a decision-making process that NASA developed during the early heyday of space exploration.

Let's apply some key decision-making principles to Adam and Nora's situation and learn how decisions can be made with a little more clarity and a lot more confidence.

1. The right question matters! It is important to ask the right question at the start. Rather than asking, "Should we move to the neighborhood up the street or stay where we are?" Nora and Adam should frame the question to ask, "What is the best housing option for our family right now?" Nora and Adam both want to find the best housing scenario for their family, and asking a broader question beyond merely "this versus that" opens up the options and helps them to think creatively. Framing the question in this light reminds them of their ultimate goal and prevents the decision from leaning toward an "either/or" trap. When mind-sets shift, Adam remembers that his parents have an empty lot near their home in a neighboring suburb, and they begin talking about building a new home there. Nora and Adam also imagine what it would be like for them to move in to the city to a neighborhood where many of their church friends are living "on mission." The final two options entered the conversation after they began to think about their housing question more broadly.

2. Compare alternatives to objectives rather than to each other. Adam and Nora begin by listing their objectives—both the unified ones and the individual ones. Their list includes "space for the kids to play," "community that happens naturally," "saving $400 monthly for retirement," "funding a savings account for Christian school," etc. Together they prioritize their objectives from most to least important. Defining their alternatives (stay in the current home, move to the nearby new home, build a home near Adam's parents, or move to the city near church friends) is important before comparing each alternative to their list of objectives in order to measure the alternative against the objectives, "scoring" each one. At the end of this process, they have a better sense of the benefits and pitfalls of each choice. Plus it's easier to make a rational decision about the options since they've taken the time to get clarity together, ahead of time.

3. Avoid common pitfalls/temptations. Below are some of the common pitfalls of decision making:

Binary Trap: Limiting alternatives to an "either/or" and not thinking creatively about other alternatives. Nora and Adam are both encouraged when they realize that they actually have many good options for their next house, if they choose to move. They had become so laser-focused on the construction happening just up the road that they hadn't thought bigger about their options until they reframed their question.

Voting Trap: Gathering opinions from too many people. It is wonderful to seek wise counsel, but polling friends to get opinions is rarely helpful! Adam and Nora schedule a dinner with some mentors that they trust. However, they resist the temptation to make every conversation with friends a conversation about their moving decision, since that would inevitably create a roller coaster of ideas and opinions that they would have to sort out.

Intuitive Trap: Relying solely on feelings. Feelings are real, but they don't always tell you the whole truth. Through this process, Adam realizes that his fear of not having enough in retirement causes him to lean toward hoarding, so he knows it's wise to set a saving goal that is reasonable and then to lay down his fear of the future, knowing he is saving wisely.

4. Apply wisdom to the decision before you implement it. "What's the worst thing that could happen and if that becomes reality, can I live with it?" is my favorite question to ask after I have made a decision. Nora and Adam's decision-making process has shown that their best alternative, on paper, is moving near Adam's parents. However, they ask themselves this question and realize that being in proximity to family would make some unhealthy family dynamics worse, and they are not willing to take that risk. Therefore, they move down the list to the "next best" decision with confidence because they are able to trust the reasoning and the process.

Making decisions in the midst of simultaneous competing priorities is never simple, but following some wise principles along the way will definitely help us to have firmer footing in our decisions!

Live

The Live wedge is the biggest wedge of our pie. It's where the rubber meets the road in financial decision making.

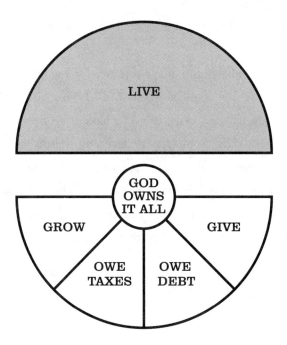

Live: *Spend less than you can because every success in your financial life depends on this habit.*

Over the years, I've had the opportunity to be on many radio call-in shows to answer people's financial questions. If I had a dollar for every question I've answered, I'd be a wealthy man! In fact, when I had the idea to write my first book thirty years ago, I mistakenly believed that if I wrote a book to answer people's questions, the book would be sufficient. I was so very wrong! Even with twenty books written by now, I continue to answer people's specific financial questions.

It turns out that every single one of us wants to be reassured in our unique financial situations. Whether we are living paycheck to paycheck or are independently wealthy, we all want to know the answer to the question, "Am I doing okay?" or "Do I have enough?"

A few years back, my oldest son asked if I would go to breakfast to talk through his financial questions. A high school teacher with a young family, he wanted me to take a look at his finances to reassure him that he was doing okay. After listening to him share his savings plan, his budgeting efforts, and his thoughts about long-term goals, I was happy to reassure him that he was doing great—way more than just "okay." My hunch is that I'd be able to have the same conversation with many of you reading this book. You're most likely doing okay, too!

Key #3: The Pie: Live

As I've shared, the path to "okay" is really just to follow the five basic money management principles. Do you remember the first one: "Spend less than you earn because everything else depends on this habit"? This principle is the key to having flexibility in your Live wedge.

But how? I believe that in order to consistently spend less than we earn, we have to learn how to make "ahead-of-time" decisions.

Let me explain.

Scripture offers us three very important guardrails concerning our Live wedge, each of which is found in the book of 1 Timothy.

The first is **provision**. "But if anyone does not provide for his own, that is his own household, he has denied the faith and is worse than an unbeliever" (1 Tim. 5:8).

The second is **contentment**. "But if we have food and clothing, we will be content with these" (1 Tim. 6:8).

The third is **enjoyment**. "For everything created by God is good, and nothing should be rejected if it is received with thanksgiving" (1 Tim. 4:4). "Instruct those who are rich in the present age not to be arrogant or to set their hope on the uncertainty of wealth, but on God, who richly provides us with all things to enjoy" (1 Tim. 6:17).

Each of these three guardrails—provision, contentment, and enjoyment—is an area where we can, and should, make ahead-of-time decisions.

Provision: How Much Is Enough?

As adults, most of us can recall a time in our early or mid-twenties when it dawned on us that our parents weren't going to show up to guide us through a particular situation. Anything from figuring out how to turn utilities on in a new home to buying a car alone for the first time to having a baby can be our wake-up moment to adulthood. The wake-up moment holds fear and freedom, both because adulthood is a whole new world and because it's now up to us!

When our kids were growing up, Judy and I had a saying that we used a lot (Remember, we had five kids, so we were big fans of parenting mantras that could be repurposed!). Whenever one of our children would have the privilege of getting a new level of freedom—a phone, a trip with friends, a car, etc.—we would remind them "with freedom comes responsibility." Now, this idea is not rocket science, but it's entirely true and 100 percent reliable. Freedom and responsibility are two sides of the same coin.

In fact, God is pointing out this fact to us in 1 Timothy 5:8 when He tells us that, as grown-ups, it is our responsibility to provide for the needs of our family.

Right away, I bet many of you are asking, thinking, or wondering about some of the following questions:

- What if I'm called to ministry and my salary just won't ever be very much?
- What does provision mean . . . is it just the basics, or is there something more to it?

92

- What about two-income families versus one-income families? How does the issue of provision play out in these scenarios?
- What about the "extras"? Does the provision umbrella include things like second homes or nice vacations?

At the heart of each of these questions is one that every adult needs to answer for himself or herself and that is: "What is provision?" Determining what provision means for you can be a big dilemma, largely because it raises the deeper and very personal question, "How much is enough?" Provision itself is relative depending on the individual. To some parents, it means private school for your children. To other parents, it means a roof over your kids' head and food on the table. To some of you it means avoiding college debt or paying cash for a car at sixteen. To others it means paying the electric bill or taking care of an aging parent in your home.

By answering "How much is enough?" and making an intentional, ahead-of-time decision about what provision looks like in our financial situation, we begin to make peace with the Live wedge of the pie. The world will always tell us that the answer is "more." More than we have today. More money. More stuff. More upgrades. More.

God's Word speaks to the issue of wealth and "more." Some key verses are very straightforward and remind us that money is a tool; it is not an end. As soon as wealth (or the pursuit of it) becomes our obsession, we are in dangerous territory.

Paul cautioned moderation when he said, "But if we have food and clothing, we will be content with these" (1 Tim. 6:8).

Jesus said that when our possessions own us, it is impossible to also be devoted to God. "No one can be a slave of two masters, since either he will hate one and love the other, or be devoted to one and despise the other. You cannot be slaves of God and of money" (Matt. 6:24).

And, while the Bible doesn't condemn wealth, it does condemn the love of wealth. "For the love of money is a root of all kinds of evil, and by craving it, some have wandered away from the faith and pierced themselves with many pains" (1 Tim. 6:10).

So, there is much wisdom in Scripture to guide us in answering, "How much is enough?" But at the end of the day, the answer to this all-important provision question is that it ultimately comes down to a faith journey between you and God.

I recently met two young men who graduated together from Harvard Business School. While there, they took a class called "God and Money" in the divinity school. They researched the "How much is enough?" question by looking at other business school graduates' level of income, their level of contentment, and their level of generosity. Along the way, both young men were deeply challenged to wrestle with the same question themselves, before the Lord. Best friends and accountability partners, each sensed God's leading in entirely different directions on the provision question. One, who had planned to enter into international business (and already had a lucrative job offer), sensed God leading him to go into ministry and to make a career of spreading the message of generosity. The other young man distinctly believed that God was leading him to take a very well-paying job, but to set a lifestyle cap from the very beginning of his career.[7]

Determining what provision means for you (i.e., knowing when enough is enough) is a very important and very personal journey, no matter where you are in your career path. If you are young, answering the question will help guide many lifestyle-related decisions down the road. If you are older, answering the question has a way of freeing you to set finish lines that allow you to pursue other God-given passions and goals.

No matter your age, answering the "How much is enough?" question as you provide for your family gives you the freedom to say *yes* to some things and *no* to others. You will be able to hear the world's inevitable "more" messages as passing static rather than letting it drown out the priorities in your life. You will be able to live in greater unity with your spouse, knowing you've agreed to the finish lines ahead of time. You will be content with what you have—the size of your pie—because you will have a conviction that runs deep.

Contentment: Choosing Satisfaction

Another key ahead-of-time decision in the Live wedge is one we've already talked about: contentment. This trait, above any other, should really be the hallmark of a mature believer's financial life.

Hebrews 13:5 (NASB) says, "Make sure that your character is free from the love of money, being content with what you have; for

He Himself has said, 'I will never desert you, nor will I ever forsake you.'"

The starting point for "enough" is defined in this verse—it is what I already have. For years I taught and wrote about the importance of the "How much is enough?" question. One day I realized that God had quantified "enough" in this verse. Enough is what I have. I can be content where I am, with what I have, because contentment is a choice. Contentment can be learned by becoming more rooted in the reality of God's nearness and provision and by living in the spiritual reality of His promise that, "I will never desert you, nor will I ever forsake you."

> When I encounter material temptations, do I discover a contented heart or a restless, discontented one?

Even the apostle Paul learned contentment along the way, and he shared his insight in Philippians and 1 Timothy. These verses are worth repeating because they help us remember that having peace in our financial circumstances is a learned trait and that wealth presents many opportunities to experience discontentment.

I don't say this out of need, for I have learned to be content in whatever circumstances I am. I know both how to have a little, and I know how to have a lot. In any and all circumstances I have learned the secret of being content—whether well fed or hungry, whether in abundance or in need. I am able to do all things through Him who strengthens me. (Phil. 4:11–13)

But godliness with contentment is a great gain. For we brought nothing into the world, and we can take nothing out. But if we have food and clothing, we will be content with these. But those who want to be rich fall into temptation, a trap, and many foolish and harmful desires, which plunge people into ruin and destruction. (1 Tim. 6:6–9)

Am I content?

This is a question that each one of us must answer. When I get alone with myself and sit with this question, what is the answer? When I encounter material temptations, do I discover a contented heart or a restless, discontented one?

A friend of mine lives right around the corner from where Judy and I lived twenty-five years ago, and I don't often go back to that part of town. As I recently drove him home on the once-familiar streets, I recognized a huge home that has been there for a long, long time. It is really more of an estate than a home. It is a beautiful, manicured, palatial home—drawing the eye every time. Passing it, I was reminded of the struggle in my younger years—the times I wrestled with wanting more and being fully aware of my discontentment. This time, I was able to see the wealth and the large homes around me and simply think to myself, *I'm content with what I have and with where I am.* I've been on this journey for a long time, and it was nice to have a reminder of how far God has brought me. Years ago, this drive would have nagged at me, pulling me toward the allure of "more." It was refreshing to be content with the lifestyle that I have now, knowing that it is enough, because it is what He has provided.

One of the main lessons I've learned on the path to contentment has to do with the paradox of prosperity, which I define as, "The more you have, the more choices you have, and the less real freedom you have."

There's a common belief (or lie) out there that a bigger home or a better car or a more impressive vacation or a lake house or enough money to retire early will bring more contentment. A cabana will make us content. Platinum status on the airline will make us content. Sunset cruises on the pontoon boat will make us content. Golf on Monday, Wednesday, and Friday will make us content. Fill in your own version of "the good life" here and imagine the possibility of escaping into it. This type of dreaming is tempting, because we always imagine our blissful moment without the concurrent complexity of the situation—without the stress that comes with the "more."

> Paradox of Prosperity: The more you have, the more choices you have, and the less real freedom you have.

In my own life, I can attest to this paradox. When Judy and I lived in a trailer while we were in graduate school, our lives were not complicated. It was relatively easy to choose the path of contentment because our options were quite limited. The stress of living, while real, was not on full-burn all the time. However, as we added children, homes, cars, educations, and even (for a time) a second home to the mix, life became more and more stressful. Choosing contentment became harder.

When we have more, we actually can feel like our freedom is restricted due to the stress of responsibility and the multitude of choices that come with having more. "More" is synonymous with stress; it is not synonymous with contentment. Contrary to popular opinion, contentment is not a pool in the backyard.

Nearly sixty years ago, author John Steinbeck recognized the paradox of prosperity at work in America. He wrote a letter to his good friend Adlai Stevenson, the United States ambassador to the United Nations. Just back from a trip abroad, Steinbeck wrote to Stevenson comparing two Christmases, one of wanting (the one he remembered from his childhood) and one of plenty (the one he was experiencing in 1959). The one of plenty he describes as follows:

> Then there is the other kind of Christmas with presents piled high, the gifts of guilty parents as bribes because they have nothing else to give. The wrappings are ripped off and the presents thrown down and at the end the child says—"Is that all?" Well, it seems to me that America now is like that second kind of Christmas. Having too many THINGS they spend their hours and money on the couch searching for a soul. A strange species we are. We can stand anything God and nature can throw at us save only plenty. *If I wanted to*

destroy a nation, I would give it too much and would have it on its knees, miserable, greedy and sick.[8] (italics mine)

There's a direct correlation between too much and discontentment, between having a lot and losing our soul. The good news, though, is that we don't have to experience the paradox of prosperity. We can all choose contentment. As Christians we can learn contentment through the power of Christ's indwelling strength, as Paul taught us in Philippians. Becoming content removes the engine of dissatisfaction from our lifestyle-related spending decisions. Deciding ahead of time that learning contentment is 100 percent worth it is an important key to making peace with the Live wedge of our financial pie.

Enjoyment: Grateful Intentionality

Paul's third guardrail for our lifestyle from 1 Timothy is enjoyment. "Instruct those who are rich in the present age not to be arrogant or to set their hope on the uncertainty of wealth, but on God, who richly provides us with all things to enjoy" (1 Tim. 6:17).

Answering "How much is enough?" ahead of time, and making an ahead-of-time decision to learn contentment naturally leads us to an increased capacity to enjoy God's gifts because we have greater capacity to recognize His provision and to take pleasure in His rich blessings.

The ability to gratefully enjoy the gifts we have—both material and nonmaterial—is one of the pleasures of being God's children, made in His image with the capacity to sense, feel, relate, and reason. He created us to be able to take in the bounty of life with pleasure and with gratitude. Sometimes, when we are doubled down solving the anxieties of life, we completely miss the chance to enjoy His provision. I find it so kind of our heavenly Father to remind us in His Word to enjoy life.

Because money is a tool to accomplish other goals and priorities, the Live wedge decisions offer us a great opportunity to enjoy our lives. We can use our money to create a memory with our family. We can use our resources to craft something beautiful in our home. We can spend money to have an adventure with friends.

Spending money to enjoy the life we've been given is a powerful way to celebrate God's provision and to be grateful in it. Will you decide today to enjoy what you've been given?

Making "Ahead of Time" a Way of Life

Answering "How much is enough?," choosing a path of contentment, and deciding to gratefully enjoy God's provision are all "under the waterline" and "why-oriented" decisions. Practicing provision, contentment, and enjoyment drive us to different, more thoughtful "above the waterline" and "how-oriented" decisions in our lifestyle spending.

I find it very useful to apply the ahead-of-time paradigm to the day-to-day mechanics of lifestyle decisions as well.

Much of the stress of our day-to-day financial decisions comes from the fact that we are sorting out our simultaneous competing priorities in the moment, making sense of them as we go. Whether we like budgeting or not, the fact is that setting constraints by deciding ahead of time what we will spend on food, clothes, vacations, housing, etc., allows us to walk more confidently as we spend money.

Personally, Judy and I have lived this ahead-of-time decision-making idea out in some big ways and some small ways.

Cars . . .

One big way that we lived this out is that Judy and I decided we would always pay cash for our cars, which meant that we had to save until we had enough to get another car. This ahead-of-time choice always helped us to make a more thoughtful and less impulsive car decision when it came time to get a new one.

Homes . . .

I have a forty-four-year-old friend who is debt free, including mortgage debt. Recently, he and his wife were driving through a new neighborhood where homes are more expensive than where they live currently. While entertaining the thought of moving, they came to the shared realization that being mortgage-free provides them a level of freedom that they would have to forfeit if they took on another mortgage. Their premade decision to eliminate their mortgage gave them a taste of financial freedom that they were not willing to give up. They realized they could live with less knowing the true value of financial flexibility.

Schools . . .

I've seen our adult children wrestle with their children's schooling decisions—private versus public, preschool versus staying at home, college funding, etc. As much as possible, it is so very wise to decide schooling parameters ahead of time and even to communicate them to your children, depending on their age. Doing so allows your family to make more balanced decisions in the heat of the moment, when many factors are often at play.

Children's Spending . . .

The ahead-of-time idea can play out in the simplest ways. We used to decide ahead of time how much our children would receive for clothes, spending, saving, gifts to friends, and giving each year. By giving them an envelope-based budgeting system and "paying" them at the first of each month, we had settled potential squabbles over shopping, social events, and so much more. Whatever was in their envelope was what they had available to spend.

I encourage you to think about your areas of greatest financial frustration or stress in the Live wedge of your pie. How could taking an ahead-of-time approach change the way you interact with that area to remove some of the tension from it?

There is great power in being proactive toward our lifestyle spending. We live in a culture that will always lure us into greater complexity, anxiety, and accumulation when it comes to our "stuff." As we learn to settle issues of provision, contentment, and enjoyment and as we decide "ahead of time" in our key places of financial stress, we will be free to tend to the other wedges of the pie with much more intentionality and success.

Takeaway

Living a financial lifestyle that embodies the three biblical guidelines from 1 Timothy—provision, contentment, and enjoyment—offers an opportunity for us to make ahead-of-time decisions.

Provision: Answer the question "How much is enough?" as it relates to the size of the Live wedge of your pie.

Contentment: Choose to be satisfied with what you have in a particular area of your life.

Enjoyment: Enjoy the gifts that God has given you more fully and intentionally.

Don't fall victim to paralysis by analysis. Seek God's wisdom, make a decision, and then move forward. Along the way continue to seek God's wisdom and adjust as He leads. Whatever your answer, write it in the Live wedge of the pie here, and move into that decision with confidence, knowing you are following biblical financial wisdom by doing so.

What ahead-of-time decision is most
pertinent to the Live wedge of your pie?

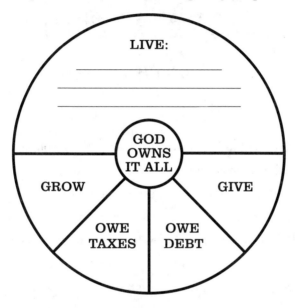

GRAHAM'S STORY

How Much Is Enough?

And Jesus said to His disciples, "Truly I say to you, it is hard for a rich man to enter the kingdom of heaven. Again I say to you, it is easier for a camel to go through the eye of a needle, than for a rich man to enter the kingdom of God." When the disciples heard this, they were very astonished and said, "Then who can be saved?" And looking at them Jesus said to them, "With people this is impossible, but with God all things are possible." (Matt. 19:23–26 NASB)

What happens when a college kid answers, "How much is enough?" before they get their first real job? In Graham Smith's case, the answer is something radical!

Mr. Smith, a Wheaton student of theology and economics, took a job on Wall Street as an investment analyst right after graduation. At Wheaton, he was a typical college student, short on money and looking forward to having more of it when working in the business world.

During his senior year, God placed several examples in Graham's path that caused him to consider what it might look like for him to live in the "real world" as a Christ follower. First, Graham heard theologian N. T. Wright speak at Wheaton. Wright discussed how Christians are called to love others even to the point of death and gave examples of Christians who lived in Asia during the plague and chose to remain in the cities to care for the sick, even though their choice often resulted in their death. Smith shares, "This was a different way to be human, and if giving away your life even to the point of death was following the way of the cross, what did this look like for me, a recent college graduate?" In addition to Wright's talk, Graham was also challenged by the example of some personal friends who served in the Middle East and loved sacrificially every day in their life and work. He couldn't quiet the questions about God, money, and "enough" that had begun swirling in his head.

Rather than keeping his questions academic, Graham set out to determine God's calling on his life as he planned his next move—a job on Wall Street. He took the summer after graduation to serve abroad and ponder his question, "How will I use my income to best glorify God in the world of abundant material wealth that I'm getting ready to enter?" By the time he moved to New York, it was with a firm conviction that God was leading him to "reverse tithe"; he lived on 10 percent of his income. Since that time, Smith finds ways to give away 90 percent of what he receives from his biweekly paycheck.

When Smith talks about his decision to give now versus saving money to give later, he says, "I used to think that I would put all of my money into investments so that I could grow them and nurture them and that way one day I could give away more. But for me, I truly believe I would view that growing net worth, that growing investment portfolio, as my own child—where I put so much effort to grow it and raise it and take care of it that when it was really big someday, I would struggle to sacrifice that child that I had raised. Investing in people lasts forever. If I don't set patterns now as a young adult, just starting my paycheck, it will never happen. This is a form of discipline of learning how to give."[9]

Graham's post-college life looked radically different from his colleagues at work. While one colleague had two apartments—one for the workweek and one for the weekend—Smith shared a one-bedroom apartment with four Christian friends. He looked for free haircuts on Craigslist and learned to give away far more than just money.

His giving journey even widened to include giving hospitality to friends passing through the city. Graham shares the gift of influence to fellow Wheaton grads by introducing them to the finance world. He also learned what it meant to give to his homeless friend Jeff, who insisted on taking nothing but friendship from Graham in an effort to preserve the boundaries and dignity of their relationship. Graham Smith's commitment has taken him far beyond the boundaries of financial giving into a lifestyle of true adventure!

Clearly, Smith is salt and light in his world. His financial decisions are a testimony of grace and generosity to a culture that is notoriously performance oriented and materialistic. He has found so much joy in "living as a 'pastor with hedge fund money.'" He wittily remarks that the best way to think about money is to see "money like manure . . . don't let it pile up but spread it around."[10]

7

Give

"Don't collect for yourselves treasures on earth, where moth and rust destroy and where thieves break in and steal. But collect for yourselves treasures in heaven, where neither moth nor rust destroys, and where thieves don't break in and steal. For where your treasure is, there your heart will be also. The eye is the lamp of the body. If your eye is good, your whole body will be full of light. But if your eye is bad, your whole body will be full of darkness. So if the light within you is darkness—how deep is that darkness! No one can be a slave of two masters, since either he will hate one and love the other, or be devoted to one and despise the other. You cannot be slaves of God and of money." (Matt. 6:19–24)

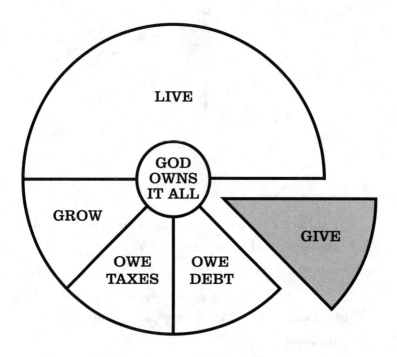

Give: *Give generously because giving breaks the power of money.*

For where your treasure is, there your heart will be also" may be Jesus' most well-known words about money. They are both mysterious and powerful, and they open up a new way to experience Kingdom life. Jesus tells us that wherever we collect treasures, our hearts always follow. Our treasures go first and our hearts follow, becoming more rooted and attached where we've chosen to invest our material wealth. The treasure principle is beautiful. A spiritual reality that can open the door to an amazing adventure with God.

Key #3: The Pie: Give

Generosity—holding money with an open hand and allowing God to use it—is the only way to become free from the grip of money.

Along the way, I've observed that an increase in money and wealth is typically followed by a decrease in generosity. There is something about abundance that causes us to tighten our grip on our money. Maybe it's fear. Maybe it's pride. Jesus knew the correlation and told us how to break the connection when He taught that our heart follows our treasure. He both modeled generosity and communicated how it is the key to breaking free from the tight grip of money.

Jesus once had an encounter with a "rich young ruler." This man approached Jesus because he wanted to know what it would take for him to inherit eternal life. They had a quick interaction about righteousness and the law and the man's good works. Then, from a place of love, Christ told the man to give his possessions to the poor and follow Him so that he would have treasure in heaven. Jesus offered him the path to true freedom. The rich young man was stunned at what Jesus said and walked away very sad because he had many possessions. He just couldn't do it.

After he left, Jesus told His disciples, "Children, how hard it is to enter the kingdom of God! It is easier for a camel to go through the eye of a needle than for a rich person to enter the kingdom of God" (Mark 10:24–25). Jesus was serving up the facts—acknowledging just how profoundly money gets in the way of a heart being fully surrendered to God.

Astonished at the harsh truth, the disciples asked the next logical question: "Then who can be saved?" and Jesus' reply was, "With men it is impossible, but not with God, because all things are possible with God" (see Mark 10:26–27).

This story offers both hope and conviction for Americans today. It shows us the difficult reality that our abundant stuff really, really gets in the way of following Christ. It also offers the powerful hope that nothing is impossible with God. He can break the power of money in our lives and He has told us how He does it. Through our generosity.

In sharing biblical truth about generosity, my goal is not to guilt you, shame you, or point a finger at you. Rather, I hope that as you consider the power of biblical generosity, you will discover the life and freedom that it can bring to your financial life and the blessing that it can offer to the world around you.

Becoming generous is like learning to swim in the ocean of grace. We ponder the grace of Jesus, we allow His grace to loosen the grip we have on our stuff, and we have the privilege of being an agent of grace in others' lives. So, consider this chapter on giving an invitation to something life changing.

A few years ago the grace of giving came home to me at a fast-food restaurant.

One morning I was at the local Chick-fil-A eating my weekly breakfast with my oldest son. Rachel regularly waited on us. She was perpetually welcoming and always greeted us with a warm smile. On this day, as I walked out of the restaurant I thought to myself, *Can*

Rachel take tips? It dawned on me that I always leave a tip in sit-down restaurants, but I never tip at fast-food places. I came back inside and asked her. In the space between my question and her answer, the Holy Spirit and I had a brief conversation.

(Me, looking at the twenties in my wallet.) "I'll be generous and give her a $20."

(The prompting of the Holy Spirit) "Ron—you cheapskate—you've got plenty of twenties. Why not give her five twenties?"

By the time she answered "yes," I had determined to give her $100 from my wallet. Folding the bills over so that she couldn't see the amount, I handed her the money and walked out, glad I had yielded to the prompting of the Holy Spirit.

The next week, I was back again for breakfast. She pulled me aside and said, "Thank you so much for the money! I needed new tires and really thought I would use your gift to buy them. But that day, my daughter came home from school and told me about a classmate who had lost everything in an apartment fire the night before. I knew that her family needed the money worse than I did, so I gave the $100 to them instead."

As we talked, Rachel went on to share more of her story. She is a mom of five children who moved to America from Central America to give her children an opportunity for a better life. She shared about her hopes for her children and bragged on her daughter, especially. Clearly, her heart was on the lookout for ways to bless her family and her community.

That day, I was deeply humbled and profoundly reminded of the power of generosity. I gave out of my abundance, and Rachel turned around and gave out of her poverty. I have a lot, and I parted with a tiny bit of it at the prompting of the Holy Spirit. She has very little, and she parted with the chance to solve a real need—tires—and took action to love her neighbor, tangibly and sacrificially. That day, I was stirred toward the grace of the Kingdom. Moving a little bit of treasure in the direction of eternity had a huge impact on my heart. Once again, I was reminded that giving breaks the power of money.

Taking Jesus at face value and becoming generous will move our hearts, as well. The reality of this truth is beautiful and undeniable. Giving always breaks the power of money, transforming our hearts in the process.

Motivations to Give

Scripture gives us many reasons to give, beyond just the treasure principle. As I've taught on giving over the years, I've identified some of the reasons that God wants us to be generous. Giving is both a multifaceted opportunity and a multifaceted blessing in our financial and spiritual lives. When we give, we are reflecting the very nature of God—His unmatched generosity—to the world around us. As those who have received His generous grace through Christ as well as the blessing of financial provision, we have the opportunity to be conduits of that grace and generosity to those who are experiencing material poverty. Understanding why we give empowers and motivates deeper generosity.

For starters, we give *out of a willing obedience to our heavenly Father*. In the Old Testament, we see tithes and offerings as integral to the care of the needy and the working of the temple.[11] In the New Testament church, there is a precedent of giving. In Acts, we read that the early believers shared readily when another believer was in need. In fact, it says that they considered what they had commonly owned by everyone else (see Acts 2:44–45). Additionally, Paul's letters to the early church encourage consistent giving: "On the first day of the week, each of you is to set something aside and save in keeping with how he prospers, so that no collections will need to be made when I come" (1 Cor. 16:2). Habitual, consistent giving is an act of obedience to God.

Giving reminds us that *God owns it all*. Living as if God is the owner of all of our resources can be hard to do in a world constantly urging us to be in control of our own lives, stuff, and money. When we give, we tangibly acknowledge that, "The earth and everything in it, the world and its inhabitants, belong to the LORD" (Ps. 24:1). When we give, we are acting as conduits of God's resources to the world, as we let them flow through our open hands to accomplish His good purposes.

Giving promises *rewards*. Scripture teaches that our actions on the earth have implications in heaven: "Remember this: The person who sows sparingly will also reap sparingly, and the person who sows generously will also reap generously. Each person should do as he has decided in his heart—not reluctantly or out of necessity, for God loves a cheerful giver" (2 Cor. 9:6–7). Also, in the Parable of the Talents, the master tells the steward, "Well done, good and faithful slave! You were faithful over a few things; I will put you in charge of many things. Share your master's joy!" (Matt. 25:23). Somehow, God connects our earthly stewardship, and in particular our giving, to eternity. Eternal rewards are in many ways mysterious, but we get a glimpse of their scope based on other Scripture. We see a hint of God's eternal "rate of return" in the Parable of the Sower where Jesus talks about seeds returning a hundredfold, sixtyfold, and thirtyfold (see Matt. 13:8). In today's terms, that's 10,000 percent, 6,000 percent, and 3,000 percent. Wow. Giving is a profound, eternal investment.

We give *because God gave*. I recently heard a story of a woman named Catherine who had saved $5,000 for a car. A woman of great faith, she worked an hourly job at a bakery and saw it as her calling to pray for her customers every day. Through her church, she became aware of a widow in need and was compelled to give this widow her entire $5,000 car fund. After sharing this with Deb, one of her regular customers, Deb and her husband decided to buy Catherine a car. They teamed up with a friend at a local car dealer and bought a new car for Catherine. Needless to say, she was blessed and blown away! In telling her story, Catherine said, "We don't give in order to receive. We give because it's the nature of Jesus Christ. He gave us His life, so we have the DNA of Jesus Christ, [the DNA] of giving."[12] Second Corinthians 8:9 summarizes the DNA of Jesus' generosity, "For you know the grace of our Lord Jesus Christ: Though He was rich, for your sake He became poor, so that by His poverty you might become rich." God's grace toward us is manifest in the extreme generosity of Jesus. God loved us so much that He *gave* His Son. We give—even to the point of extreme generosity—in response to God's unmatched generosity to us.

Our Heart Reflecting God's Heart

If the Lord wants to use giving to transform our hearts, we need to ask the question, "What is on God's heart?" Understanding what is important to the heart of God helps us to decide where to give. As we give in areas important to Him, our hearts are transformed to mirror His. I like to answer the "where give?" question by looking at three key areas that God cares about—the local church, the spread of the gospel, and care for the vulnerable.

> We give in response to God's unmatched generosity to us.

God's heart is for His bride, the church. From the beginning, the local church has been a place where believers share their resources in order to care for the leaders and to support its function—the spread of the gospel to the world. Galatians 6:6 simply states, "The one who is taught the message must share all his good things with the teacher." Part of being in the body of Christ means giving financial resources to help it to function, grow, and flourish in its mission to glorify God and share hope in the world, both locally and globally.

God's heart is to reach the world with the gospel. When Jesus left earth, He gave the Great Commission. "Then Jesus came near and said to them, 'All authority has been given to Me in heaven and on earth. Go, therefore, and make disciples of all nations, baptizing them in the name of the Father and of the Son and of the Holy Spirit, teaching them to observe everything I have commanded you. And remember, I am with you always, to the end of the age'" (Matt. 28:18–20). Fulfilling the Great Commission is God's desire for His church on the earth. When we give toward its accomplishment, we align our hearts with God's.

And, God's heart is for the vulnerable. Former Yale professor Nicholas Wolterstorff has identified what he calls "the quartet of the vulnerable"[13] in Scripture. While the four groups are mentioned throughout Scripture in various places, Zechariah 7:9–10 mentions all four groups in one verse: "This is what the Lord Almighty said: 'Administer true justice; show mercy and compassion to one another. Do not oppress the **widow** or the **fatherless**, the **foreigner** or the **poor**'" (NIV, emphasis mine). When we give to these groups, we are caring for the "least of these" (Matt. 25:40) and responding to God's love in our own lives by loving others. First John 3:17 asks, "If anyone has this world's goods and sees his brother in need but closes his eyes to his need—how can God's love reside in him?"

> God's heart is for the vulnerable.

Using our financial abundance to help the vulnerable flourish identifies us as followers of Christ and is a powerful way to pour the love of God into the world.

Prioritizing Giving

Advising clients and walking with many of them on their journey of generosity has been my distinct pleasure. Through their lives, I have witnessed how an understanding that God owns it all and that His resources are in my life for His purposes can lead people on an exciting journey of financial generosity that yields true heart-level freedom.

Since giving is the most powerful and eternally important thing we can do with our money, we are wise when we prioritize it first in our spending. To do this, we have to become very intentional about our giving and the things on which we spend money.

Do you remember when we talked about the default priorities of money versus God's priorities of money? We saw the reality that the pie wedges at the top of our priority list get the most resources, and that diminishing resources as we go down the priority order results in pressure at the bottom.

Prioritizing a generous life means knowing how to give and how much to give. It means being acquainted with the various "levels" of generosity and what they entail. Proportionate, planned, and pre-committed are the three levels of giving. Sometimes I call these levels "should give," "could give," and "would give."

Proportionate Giving

The idea of proportionate giving ("should give") is analogous to the Old Testament tithe. In the New Testament, proportionate giving comes from 1 Corinthians 16:2, which says, "On the first day of the week, each of you is to set something aside and save in keeping with how he prospers, so that no collections will need to be made when I come."

Proportionate giving means that we decide ahead of time to set aside the "firstfruits" of our income. As Paul says, we habitually give "in keeping with" how we prosper. The tithe is a starting point for being financially generous.

As a financial planner, it has always been natural for me to figure out my tithe based on 10 percent of my projected income, put it on a weekly payment schedule, and sign up to give online with my church's online giving platform. A few years ago, however, I read Robert Morris's book *The Blessed Life* and was challenged to think about my tithe—proportionate giving—in a new way. I was convicted that Judy and I were missing something by tithing in such a rote way, so we changed how we tithe. Now, on Sunday morning of every week, if we've received any income that week, I write our tithe check proportionate to the amount we've received. Then, Judy signs it and puts it in the offering plate. This new habit has been a great move for us in a few key ways. It is a weekly reminder of how blessed we are. Beyond that, it has totally opened up our communication about our income and how we use it. Better yet, doing it this way has caused us to give even more!

As Judy and I have prioritized giving more and more over the years, the proportion that we give has increased. We love to plan for a new year and decide that we can increase our giving by a certain percentage. As a couple, we practice tithing 10 percent to our church and then setting our "offerings" beyond that proportion, giving to missionaries, ministries, etc., above and beyond our tithe.

Wherever you are in your giving, I encourage you to start somewhere— decide to begin at the beginning, setting aside some portion of your income to give away on a regular basis to your church and to Kingdom work. This step not only aligns your heart with God's heart, it also reorders your financial life in alignment with biblically wise financial priorities.

> Start somewhere. Set aside some portion of your income to give away on a regular basis to your church.

Planned Giving

In 2 Corinthians 8:1–15, Paul talks about giving. He is speaking to the Corinthian church about its pledge a year earlier to give money to the Jerusalem collection, a specific offering to help the church in Jerusalem get through a time of economic hardship due to famine.[14] Paul was now finishing his collection of this offering, but the Corinthian commitment had not yet been fulfilled. In this passage, Paul appeals to them by sharing the example of the Macedonian church. The Macedonians had also pledged and contributed to the Jerusalem collection, giving out of their own extreme poverty. It's a powerful story of giving with several inherent lessons.

> We want you to know, brothers, about the grace of God granted to the churches of Macedonia: During a severe testing by affliction, their abundance of joy and their deep poverty overflowed into the wealth of their generosity. I testify that, on their own, according to their ability and beyond their ability, they begged us insistently for the privilege of sharing in the ministry to the saints, and not just as we had hoped. Instead, they gave themselves especially to the Lord, then to us by God's will. So we urged Titus that just as he had begun, so he should also complete this grace to you. Now as you excel in everything—faith, speech, knowledge, and in all diligence, and in your love for us—excel also in this grace.
>
> I am not saying this as a command. Rather, by means of the diligence of others, I am testing the genuineness of your love. For you know the grace of our Lord Jesus Christ: Though He was rich, for your sake He became poor, so that by His poverty you might become rich. Now I am giving an opinion on this because it is profitable for you, who a year ago began not only to do something but also to desire it. But now finish the task as well, that just as there was eagerness to desire it, so there may also be a completion *from what you have*. For if the eagerness is there, it is acceptable *according*

to what one has, not according to what he does not have. It is not that there may be relief for others and hardship for you, but it is a question of equality—at the present time *your surplus is available for their need,* so their abundance may also become available for our need, so there may be equality. As it has been written: The person who gathered much did not have too much, and the person who gathered little did not have too little. (2 Cor. 8:1–15, emphasis mine)

I define planned giving as giving out of what you have. In the Scripture above, Paul urged the Corinthians to give what they had planned to give—to give out of what they had.

This type of giving is above and beyond the proportionate giving of a tithe. It stems from having answered the all-important question, "How much is enough?" and then giving out of the excess or the margin. When we look at needs around us—in the church, in ministries, in the life of a missionary, sometimes God puts it on our heart to give something we already have. Perhaps we give something tangible—a car or furniture. Or, perhaps we give some savings that we had set aside for something else—a home improvement, a vacation, etc.—to meet a need according to the conviction of the Holy Spirit. This type of giving is what some might call "sacrificial giving" because we are "sacrificing" something we've earmarked for another purpose by giving it away instead.

It is easy to miss the opportunity to give out of what we already have—it doesn't even occur to us to give what is already in our stash of stuff! Engaging in planned giving means adopting a new way of thinking—it means looking at what we have accumulated and considering the gifts that could come out of those accumulations rather than just viewing giving as an income-based decision.

One year when our children were young, Judy and I made a giving pledge to a ministry. When it came time to give, our cash flow was less than I had anticipated, and we did not have the money in the natural flow of our proportionate giving to be able to meet the pledge. The money we did have available was our summer vacation fund—it nearly exactly matched the amount we'd pledged to give. One day I was reading this passage from 2 Corinthians. When I got to the part about completing the task that was pledged a year ago, I stopped, as this seemed to be written directly to me about the giving pledge we had made. Judy and I agreed that we would meet the pledge and give up our family vacation that summer.

This is an example of planned giving—we had planned to give "above and beyond," and we used resources already in our possession to do the giving, even when it put a pinch on our "Live" wedge.

Amazingly, God in His grace provided not one but three all-inclusive vacations for our family that year. In fact, we did not pay for a vacation for years after that experience. I will never, ever forget the way that God's generosity far exceeded ours! Don't miss the joy that comes from considering your total financial picture and realizing that there is far more to giving than just a percentage of income!

Precommitted Giving

The final "level" of giving is what I call precommitted or "would give" generosity. This is a faith gift that says, "God, if You would provide me a certain amount, I will give it."

Precommitted giving does not obligate God, but it recognizes that if God chooses to bless me, I will give that blessing in a particular way.

It is rare in our world of abundance that people engage God about giving in this way. When they do, and when He meets them in that place of faith, the outcome is powerful! In the passage above, the Macedonians gave "beyond their ability" to the Jerusalem collection, setting an example of faith for other churches like the Corinthians.

When our children were elementary school aged, our church hosted a mission conference. While there, one of our daughters pledged to give $2 per week for the entire year. When she made the pledge, Judy and I cringed internally, because her allowance was only $1 per week at the time. Somehow, every week, our daughter put $2 into the offering plate. I suppose I could have gone back and found out where the money came from—maybe it was her birthday money or maybe it was babysitting income—but she always had the money to give. She always had twice her weekly income to put in the plate. We were never quite sure how it happened, but the Lord met her faith with an increase, and she met her pledge.

At the end of the day, giving is one of the most amazing privileges of being a believer. It is always transformational for us and for the recipient because it puts His character and goodness on display.

God's grace is more than we can ask, think, or imagine. Through His generosity, He made a way for us to share in the power of giving, laying up treasure in heaven and allowing us to be conduits of His grace to the world.

Takeaway

God wants us to be good stewards of His resources and use them for His purposes. What would it look like to be a conduit of God's grace to a broken world through giving?

What I should give: _____

What I could give by making a sacrifice
in a certain area: _____

What I would give if God blesses me
with this amount: _____

I WILL GIVE: _____

Ask the Lord for wisdom and direction as you seek, by His grace, to break the hold money has on you in a particular area.

Owe Debt

Debt.

Does the word make your palms sweaty? Or does it make your stomach drop?

We have arrived at the challenging part, friends, and we're going to tackle it head-on. You can do it.

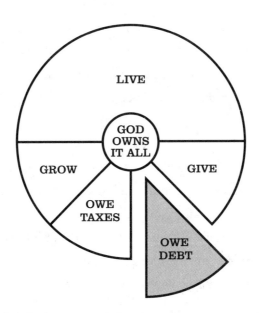

Debt: *Avoid debt because debt always mortgages the future.*

Key #3: The Pie: Debt

Financial stress and debt are synonymous for many of us. Some live with a low hum of debt stress that is "manageable." Others are contending with a full-on roar of debt that threatens to overwhelm, creating terrible credit scores, lost dreams, or fractured relationships.

Debt is an uncomfortable reality for a majority of Americans.

The United States government releases a debt analysis based on its census data every ten years. In their analysis of personal debt in America between 2000 and 2011, the following trends were true:

The Good News: A growing number of people are getting out of debt entirely. The percentage of households with debt dropped from 74.2 percent to 69.0 percent between 2000 and 2011.

The Bad News: People with debt tend to have growing debt loads. The median amount of total debt held by households in debt went up from $50,971 to $70,000, and the median amount of unsecured debt (credit card, student, etc.), rose from $5,365 to $7,000.

The Demographic News: The age group with the largest increase in unsecured debt was people under age forty-five.[15] And, ironically, as someone's education level increases, so does the percentage of people in that demographic willing to take on credit card debt.[16]

So, if you're a highly educated person under forty-five, that means that, statistically speaking, you are probably carrying a heavy load of debt and you are likely living and working among peers with the same problem. No matter your age or your education level, you are not alone if you struggle with debt.

Debt Is Symptomatic

Five years ago, I had a heart problem and did not know it.

My blood pressure was normal, I felt fine, and I was moving quickly through the activities of my life, unaware that my heart was poised to experience a massive, "widow-maker" heart attack. I was a ticking time bomb.

After I had a few palpitations and some shortness of breath, I visited the cardiologist. When he did a procedure to look at my heart, he scheduled me for open-heart surgery . . . the next day. Four bypasses and a very long recovery period later, I was a new man. I had not known that my energy level was low until my heart was free to work like it did decades ago. I felt so much better!

My minor symptoms were indicators of a much deeper problem.

Debt, even when it's the nagging "low hum" variety, is symptomatic of deeper issues.

We've said before that money issues are heart issues. Debt is a money issue telling us that something in our heart is resulting in a problem in our wallet.

So, while you could easily Google "get out of debt" and have any number of debt reduction strategies, blogs, budget trackers, or apps appear, ready to walk you through legitimate debt elimination plans, I want to ask you to first consider that debt is a symptom of something else and look a little deeper at its root cause in your life.

A debt problem is like driving a car at full speed with a funny noise in the engine. If we keep driving, ignoring the rattle, we are poised for a major crash. The wise idea is to slow down, stop the car, examine the rattle, and find the problem. We can't fix our financial mess or the heart issue behind it if we don't first stop to diagnose it and then deal with it. It's worth a bit of delay to fix what is really the problem—for our wallets and our hearts. Solving the root cause of our financial problem prevents the cycle of slowing down just long enough to quiet the rattle only to hear it again when we get back up to the speed of life, leaving us in a similar situation down the road.

I'll bet that if you stop to think about it, you could articulate some of the heart issues that are behind the debt in your life.

Over my career, I've interacted with people at every income level in every level of debt imaginable. Sometimes debt indicates a prevailing lack of contentment. Often it reveals a lack of self-discipline or pride. Other times it is motivated by a desire to be accepted. Debt can reveal someone's need to control a certain situation or be a symptom of short-term thinking over long-term planning. What could be the "heart" behind your debt?

Whatever your "rattle," there is grace in Christ to face it head-on and to overcome it. Once you have identified the root of your debt problem you can effectively put into practice one of many debt-reduction strategies. Having a good understanding of debt—principles about it, dangers in it, and reasons to use it—will guide your decision making and will help you guard your heart as you tackle your debt.

Principles of Scripture

The Bible has some straightforward things to say about debt.

Debt enslaves us. "The rich rule over the poor, and the borrower is a slave to the lender" (Prov. 22:7). Debt obligates us—deeply—to the point of being a "slave" to the one who has loaned us money. When we have debt, we owe the lender first. In reality, we work to pay that lender before we work to pay for anything else in the Live, Give, or Grow wedges of our pie.

Debt must be repaid. The alternative to repaying debt is tangible, material loss. "Don't be one of those who enter agreements, who put up security for loans. If you have no money to pay, even your bed will be taken from under you" (Prov. 22:26–27).

There is a real cost to borrowing. While debt seems "easy" in the moment, it always costs us—more and later. We pay dearly for today's desires because we pay using tomorrow's income, but with the added burden of interest on top. Debt is an easy path to a harder tomorrow. Jesus warned against dismissing the real cost of our choices when He said, "For which of you, wanting to build a tower, doesn't first sit down and calculate the cost to see if he has enough to complete it? Otherwise, after he has laid the foundation and cannot finish it, all the onlookers will begin to make fun of him, saying, 'This man started to build and wasn't able to finish.' Or what king, going to war against another king, will not first sit down and decide if he is able with 10,000 to oppose the one who comes against him with 20,000?" (Luke 14:28–31).

Debt presumes on the future. We cannot know what the future holds. When we choose debt, we place undue confidence in an unknown future. James 4:13–16 warns against this type of presumption. "Come now, you who say, 'Today or tomorrow we will travel to such and such a city and spend a year there and do business and make a profit.' You don't even know what tomorrow will bring—what your life will be! For you are like smoke that appears for a little while, then vanishes. Instead, you should say, 'If the Lord wills, we will live and do this or that.' But as it is, you boast in your arrogance. All such boasting is evil."

> When we choose debt, we place undue confidence in an unknown future.

Debt Is Not a Sin

While the Bible says a lot about debt, it does not say that debt is a sin or that it is morally wrong. It says that debt is dangerous. Debt is rarely a financially wise decision, but Scripture does not say that all debt is wrong.

> The Bible says that debt is dangerous.

Before we talk about what a "good" debt decision looks like, I'd like to share some of the dangers of debt—some very real ways that debt weakens or compromises us.

134

Economic Dangers

The most obvious danger of debt is the simple economic reality that debt mortgages the future. Debt always costs more to get out of than to get into. This high future cost is evident in a few key ways.

First, debt obligates tomorrow's income. We are effectively saying, "I will earn money tomorrow so that I can have something today." So, even if debt carries no interest at all (which sometimes happens when we get a "deal" and get zero percent interest), we still bind ourselves to earning money in the future to pay for today's stuff. This obligation also means that tomorrow's financial margin for spending on tomorrow's wants and needs will be reduced.

Second, when we borrow to buy, we are effectively borrowing "before tax" money. The $25,000 I borrow on my new car represents a future income of more than $25,000. Taking out a car loan of this amount means I will have to earn future income, pay taxes on it, and THEN pay back the $25,000 loan on my car. So, depending on my tax bracket, the $25,000 of debt may put a $30,000, $35,000, or even higher strain on my economic future, since I will have to earn the income, pay the income taxes on it, and then pay the debt. In other words, there will be $30,000–$35,000 of my future income that will not be available for anything else.

Finally, when we have debt, we are allowing the magic of compounding to work against us rather than for us. The magic of compounding is a really amazing financial principle that works by the continual reinvestment of our investment or interest gains over long stretches of time. For example, if a person invests $5,000 annually for ten years, between ages twenty-five and thirty-five at an annual return of 7 percent, they will have over $600,000 available at age sixty-five on that original $50,000 investment, even without investing anything more between ages thirty-five and sixty-five.[17] Remarkable and true!

This powerful financial "magic" works against us in debt situations. For example, a $15,000 credit card debt at 18 percent interest could require paying back almost four times the amount borrowed if a person only makes the minimum payment. The credit card company gets away with this because they are earning interest on the original amount borrowed and on the interest that is accruing on that person's unpaid balance. The borrower ends up paying interest on interest.

The opportunity cost of consumption—the reality of paying principal and interest toward debt now rather than saving it and earning interest on it in the future—is very costly. If I am paying $5,000 in debt per year rather than saving that $5,000 and earning interest on it (as in the savings example above), I am effectively giving up the future opportunity for $600,000 in savings. The banker—the lender—is the one getting the good end of the deal while the borrower—me—gets the costly end of the deal.

Debt is easy (far too easy) to get into and very, very hard to get out of. The economic realities of debt make tomorrow's financial future much less free. Simply put, today's debt puts a heavy burden on tomorrow's flexibility.

Psychological Dangers

Anyone who has struggled with debt knows that debt is also psychologically stressful. Studies show that debt can lead to health problems and relational strain. A few years ago, researchers at Southampton University looked at sixty-five published studies on debt and demonstrated that debt stress is correlated to mental health issues, especially depression.[18] Also, 64 percent of graduate students report that constant concern over debt interferes with optimal functioning.[19] On the physical health front, an Ohio State study showed that there is a link between the worst health cases and high levels of credit card debt. A study in the journal of *Social Science and Medicine* showed that young people with financial debt also report higher blood pressure.[20] Debt causes stress. Stress and poor mental and physical health are linked.

The other kind of stress that debt can create is relational stress. I can't tell you how many client meetings I have led where debt issues were creating tension. Even normal mortgage debt can be a cause of disagreement and tension in a marriage. Debt elevates the collective blood pressure in a relationship.

Researcher and professor Sonya Britt of Kansas State University studied the relationship between financial stress and marital struggle. She reported, "In the study, we controlled for income, debt and net worth. . . . Results revealed it didn't matter how much you made or how much you were worth. Arguments about money were the top predictor for divorce because it happens at all levels."[21] Confirming her findings, another study revealed that "large amounts of debt have severe effects on a household's psychological well-being."[22]

Spiritual Dangers

Debt can be spiritually dangerous for those of us who are seeking to follow Christ and to trust God as owner and provider.

As we have already discussed, borrowing always presumes on the future. This presumption is spiritually dangerous—Scripture calls it "arrogance" (James 4:16). Micah 6:8 says, "Mankind, He has told you what is good and what it is the LORD requires of you: to act justly, to love faithfulness, and to walk humbly with your God." Going into debt, arrogantly assuming that tomorrow will hold the same or increased levels of financial ability, leads us away from a humble, daily walk of contentment with our God.

Another spiritual danger of debt is that it may deny God an opportunity to provide. Almost forty years ago I started Ronald Blue & Co., a Christian financial advising firm. I needed some working capital to get the business going. I secured a line of credit from a local bank for $10,000. As I prayed through the various aspects of starting the business, I was less and less comfortable with relying on debt, so I called the bank to cancel the line not knowing the implications for my fledgling endeavor. It was a risky move—I had no clients, an unproven business, and few personal financial resources. About a week later, I was networking at an international company head-quartered in my hometown of Atlanta. One of the training directors asked if I had any interest in developing a financial planning seminar for them. At the time, I was in the midst of developing this type of seminar as the basis for my new business, so I eagerly agreed. When I asked him what he would pay, he thought it over and replied, "We can pay you $6,000 to develop the seminar and $4,000 to teach it four times in the next year."

God had $10,000 for me. It came in a very unexpected way. I have no way of knowing whether I would have still been given the opportunity to develop and teach the seminar if I had kept my line of credit, but I believe it is no coincidence that God provided the exact amount of my cancelled line of credit when I took the step of faith and relied on Him rather than on debt.

In another instance, I counseled a seminary student who called into a radio program asking whether I thought it was a good idea for him to take out student loans to get his degree. He intended to eventually serve as a missionary overseas, so I knew that his future income would be very stressed if he had to pay back a loan. I suggested that if God had called him to be a missionary, God would also provide the funds along the way. Accordingly, I challenged him to rely on God's provision rather than on debt.

A few years later, I got a letter from this young man. He told me that he had taken my advice and decided not to get loans. To complete his seminary degree, he worked several jobs, received unexpected gifts, and had many, many stories of God's unique provision for him along the way. He not only graduated debt free, but he had also experienced God's faithfulness in up-close and personal ways.

Faith-based financial decisions open the door for us to see God "do His thing" and work powerfully as owner and provider of our resources. Taking on debt can obscure our vision and short-circuit this amazing growth opportunity!

A Good Debt Decision

So what is a good debt decision? Understanding all of the dangers of debt helps us come up with solid criteria for making a "good" debt decision.

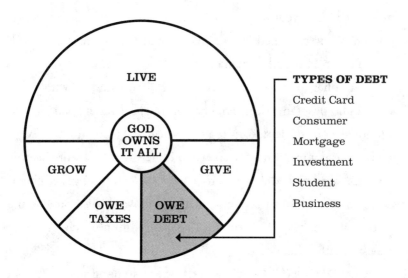

In the overall category of debt, there are six different kinds of debt: credit card debt, consumer debt, mortgage debt, investment debt, student debt, and business debt. Some are more dangerous than others. The following criteria help us to walk wisely into a debt decision:

1. The economic return is greater than the economic cost and there is a guaranteed way of repayment. (Economic criteria)

Action step #1: Run the numbers to see whether the cost to borrow (after tax interest) is less than the economic benefit (interest, yield, future value, growth in asset, etc.).

Action step #2: Specifically identify the guaranteed way to repay the debt.

2. You and your spouse (if applicable) are free from anxiety about the decision and are unified in it. (Psychological criteria)

Action step #1: Pray.

Action step #2: Talk with others affected by the decision.

Action step #3: Seek counsel.

Action step #4: Decide.

3. There is spiritual peace of mind and the decision does not violate biblical principles. (Spiritual criteria)

Action step #1: Meet with God about the decision specifically, seeking His will.

Action step #2: Meet with a wise counselor if there's a lack of clarity about whether the decision violates biblical principles.

4. The debt provides a solution for goals and objectives that can't be met in any other obvious way, such as a medical emergency, job loss, or some other financial issue that is unforeseen and unavoidable.

Action step #1: Clarify the specific goal being met in the midst of the emergency situation.

Action step #2: Explore all other possible solutions.

In the list above, criteria two through four are worked out between my spouse, God, and me as we walk through the specific goals, objectives, and constraints that give context to the debt decision at hand.

However, criteria number one is quite objective, so I have applied it to a few debt scenarios here to explain it more fully.

In the cases of *consumer debt and credit card debt*, there is always a clear violation of criteria number one. Consumer and credit card debt never pay for items or assets that will yield an economic benefit down the road. It makes zero economic sense for me to pay 18 percent extra for a dinner that is consumed in the moment or for me to pay over twenty-four months at a low interest rate for an electronic gadget that will depreciate immediately when I walk out of the store. By the same token, if I borrow to buy a car, even at zero interest, when I drive the car off the lot, I am worse off financially.

Recently, I counseled a fifty-four-year-old man at my church who was spending 22 percent of his income on debt repayment to pay for his "toys"—items that were decreasing in value and for which he was paying between 12 percent and 20 percent interest. His motorcycle, boat, RV, etc., were consuming his financial margin, and he still owed $108,000 in student debt as well. Even though the value of his "toys" were not worth enough to back his debt, I counseled him to sell them, take the losses, and pay the debt as quickly as possible.

By doing so, he was getting himself out of the kind of debt that only serves to consume today's resources to pay for yesterday's desires.

The economic cost versus the economic return for mortgage, student, investment, and business debt can be a different story.

Let's consider *student debt*. If I am planning toward a degree in a field that has good job opportunities with strong salaries, I can reasonably assume that the economic reward of using some level of debt to pay for my degree is greater than the economic cost. Today's debt facilitates tomorrow's career and that career will provide enough for me to comfortably pay the debt. Sometimes, though, if I am pursuing a very costly degree to get a job in a field with lower pay, the future economic return really may not be worth the economic cost today. In both scenarios, I need to consider whether I have some guaranteed way to repay the debt in the future—my salary, a gift from parents or grandparents, etc.

In the case of *mortgage debt*, the first criteria can be tricky, given the shifting housing market today. In general, I tend to think that putting a solid amount down (at least 20 percent, to protect against market downturns) and being in a housing market that is holding steady or growing allows me to meet criteria number one based on the fact that I can pay my mortgage by giving the bank back my house in a worst-case scenario. Also, with a low interest rate and a housing market trending toward appreciation, my economic return is likely greater than my economic cost.

A common pitfall with housing is for people to buy more house than they should, believing that their home is an "investment." When we call a home an investment, we are really justifying our purchase, because an investment is something we intend to sell as soon as it reaches some predetermined value. We don't usually buy our homes with this strategy in mind. We buy them to live in—a home is a lifestyle decision, not an investment decision. A home may end up having been a good purchase, but I never call a home an investment! Home ownership requires a lot of time, effort, and money. Purely from a perspective standpoint, it can be wise to think of a home as a liability—likely to cost us more than we anticipate—in order to make a wise home purchase.

With business and investment debt, situations are very unique. Taking a realistic view of criteria number one and looking hard at the numbers to analyze the likely future prospects of the decision are very, very important steps when deciding whether a debt decision is also a good decision.

You Can Do It

Debt is a heavy topic. It's the wedge of the pie that crowds the others and restricts us from spending according to our priorities and goals in the Live, Give, and Grow wedges.

Think about the possibilities. Say you're paying 10 percent of your total pie toward debt. Now imagine that wedge of your pie being gone altogether. The possibilities are significant—your Live wedge could grow, your Give wedge could grow, and your Grow wedge could grow. If you used some of that money to give more, your tax deductions would increase, shrinking your Owe Taxes wedge, too. Opening up space in your pie begins with eliminating the Owe Debt wedge. Eliminating debt is the quickest way to more margin, flexibility, and freedom in your financial picture.

> Eliminating debt is the quickest way to more margin, flexibility, and freedom in your financial picture.

You can do it. You can get out of debt. Lately I've been involved in a partnership with some Christian universities developing curriculum and working on research initiatives in the personal finance space. Through these relationships, I've had the privilege of getting to know the university world more closely. I have seen firsthand that student debt is one of the most burdensome types of debt—young people don't often realize just how heavy carrying a debt load can be. They often struggle to start their adult life on firm financial footing because they have taken on more debt than they can reasonably handle after graduation. Aggressively addressing the repayment of student and consumer debt is one of the best things a young person can do to care for their long-term financial health.

I heard an encouraging story of one young man, Jordan Arnold, who graduated with $23,150 in student debt. In his own words, "In the fall semester of my senior year, I remember being kind of nervous. I knew I had to start paying my debt within six months. It's stressful, when you don't have any money. And I heard all these stories about college students who get out of school, they have all this debt, and they can't find jobs. Getting my debts paid off was important to me. I didn't want to get to the point where I'd have to be paying student loans for another 10 years. Right now, I'm single. I don't have any dependents that rely on my income. But I didn't want to have these loans over my head when I'm trying to feed a family and put a roof over their heads. It's not just about me, it's about my future family."[23]

In order to pay his debt, Arnold, a finance major, decided to move home after he graduated, where he could live rent-free. He was employed at an insurance agency and added a job as a pizza delivery guy in the evenings. Working seventy-five to eighty hours a week allowed him to pay off his debt in ten months' time.

His advice to students in the same situation is this, "If you have a game plan, you can accomplish your goals. I have an account on Mint.com, that's where I kept my budget. That's a big part of it—just seeing your progress and knowing you're getting closer. Also, have an emergency fund. While I was paying off that debt, I had a small car accident. I was delivering a pizza, and I hit something in someone's driveway. It cost me about $760 to fix the car. But I had a $1,000 emergency fund, which was kind of a buffer that I kept because life happens. Finally, don't be afraid to move home if you have to. That was a big part of how I got out of debt."

My deepest respect goes to Jordan and to many others who are working diligently to pay off debt right now. I can promise you with certainty that your journey is worth it and that God stands ready with wisdom and provision to aid you in your journey out of debt.

Takeaway

Do you have a debt you would like to repay? Do you have a plan to keep you on track and a partner to encourage you when you want to give up?

Creating a plan can be as straightforward as determining the debt you have with the highest interest rate and allocating a certain extra amount to the repayment of that debt—small amounts add up over time. When that debt is repaid, you roll the total of what you were paying on that first debt toward the debt with the second highest interest rate. And so forth. Momentum will build and what once seemed impossible will suddenly seem possible.

Choose a partner who will tell you the truth, follow through with checking in on your progress regularly, and encourage you along the way.

If you don't carry a debt load, congratulations! I encourage you to be open to walking closely with a friend who is carrying a heavy debt load, as their encourager and supporter along the way.

BETH'S STORY

Tackling Debt Head-On

Wow, Beth thought, *I was ten years old when I opened my savings account!* Her savings account was her mom's idea as part of budgeting her allowance. She would tithe ten percent, save ten percent, and spend the rest at her discretion. Beth says, "While my mom's actions may have seemed small at the time, they led me to set three key financial goals: responsibly pay college tuition and student loans within two years of graduating, buy a car in full, and work in a career with benefits that I enjoyed."

Once she decided to attend Indiana Wesleyan University and received her student financial aid package, Beth set a specific financial goal: to graduate with no more than $15,000 in debt.

Today, in her mid-twenties, Beth has accomplished her original goals. As she reflected on what it took to pay for college and get out of debt within two years of graduation, she shared several things she learned in the process.

1. *Set a Goal:* Beth watched the challenges her older siblings faced as they paid for their college tuitions and recognized

that she would need to be intentional to be able to afford college.

2. *Plan Early:* Beth began saving her money in high school (even quarters for laundry money!) and researched the schools and financial aid options that were the best fit.

3. *Budget:* Beth said, "A budget is a visual . . . you don't have to follow it strictly but having one helps you gauge where you are." An important part of Beth's budget was her emergency fund that kept her from getting off track when unexpected expenses came up.

4. *Prioritize:* Along with paying for college, Beth also wanted to prioritize building strong relationships. In college, she often weighed her opportunities, deciding that investing time and money was worth it when the investment led to stronger relationships. She remarked, "In society today, we want to have everything. The reality is that we can't have everything. You have to decide ahead of time what is important and what are you willing to give up now so that you can have something later."

5. *Work Consistently:* During college, Beth worked ten to twenty-five hours per week for four years, putting fifty percent of her income toward the "college tuition" portion of her budget. At graduation, her debt was $16,000—only $1,000 more than her goal.

6. *Ask Questions and Make Adjustments:* After graduating, Beth realized that the rules on one of her loans had changed,

meaning that she was unknowingly accruing interest already, even during the grace period. She had to ask questions, but once she understood, she changed her strategy and kept at it, focusing her attention on this loan first. She admits, "Sometimes we're embarrassed to even seek out help, ask questions, or even say, 'Hey, what do I need to be asking?' It takes a step of faith to put ourselves out there a bit and ask questions of people."

7. *Acknowledge Pride:* Beth doesn't think that people would look at her and say, "You're really prideful," but she shared that during college it was often a blow to her pride to have to say no to things. "When you get invited to do something you want to say yes because you want to look good," Beth remarked. She also struggled with pride during the few months she lived with her mom, not wanting people to assume she was irresponsible even though she did pay her mom rent. "It really came down to realizing when I needed to be humbled a little bit."

8. *Trust God's Goodness:* Reflecting back, Beth says, "God continues to amaze me, and I hope that as I hear God's small voice whispering, 'Do you trust Me? Have peace and rest in Me,' that I will hold fast to His amazing love. To God be the glory."

9

Owe Taxes

Then they sent some of the Pharisees and the Herodians to Him to trap Him by what He said. When they came, they said to Him, "Teacher, we know You are truthful and defer to no one, for You don't show partiality but teach truthfully the way of God. Is it lawful to pay taxes to Caesar or not? Should we pay, or should we not pay?" But knowing their hypocrisy, He said to them, "Why are you testing Me? Bring Me a denarius to look at." So they brought one. "Whose image and inscription is this?" He asked them. "Caesar's," they said. Then Jesus told them, "Give back to Caesar the things that are Caesar's, and to God the things that are God's." And they were amazed at Him. (Mark 12:13–17)

Taxes are a reality. In fact, of all of our pie wedges, they are the reality that we have the least control over. We can plan well, but we are more or less obligated to a certain amount of taxes, particularly when it comes to income.

Key #3: The Pie: Taxes

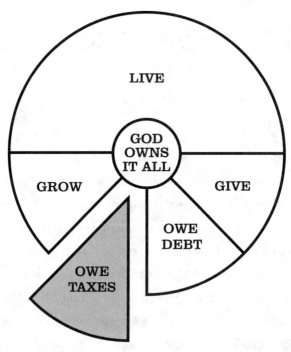

Taxes: *Pay taxes with gratitude because they indicate God's provision.*

As I think about taxes, I remember our iceberg example. What's under the waterline matters so much when it comes to taxes. Our perspective, our beliefs, and our convictions about why we pay taxes and how those realities reflect our relationship to God and to government is very important. The "tip of the iceberg" may not be very flexible, but the massive heart issues below the waterline are powerful, and even encouraging. My hope as I share some perspective and insight on taxes with you is that the tax "pill" becomes potentially less bitter to swallow and you can better enjoy what taxes represent, below the surface of their often frustrating reality.

Resentment is one of the most prevailing sentiments toward paying taxes. Why? We simply don't like giving the government a portion of our hard-earned income! Remembering that God owns it all is the first step to getting over our resentment about paying our taxes. As taxpayers who are also Christians, we represent our heavenly Father and His views about taxes to the world.

Taxes Are Symptomatic

When we talked about debt, we discussed how debt is symptomatic of something deeper—a heart issue—related to how we think about and use our money. In a similar way, taxes are symptomatic, too. However, taxes are actually symptomatic of something characteristic of God's heart toward us: His provision.

If we did not have an income or the means to buy things that are accompanied by taxes, each of us would be in a far, far worse place. We pay taxes because we have means. God is providing for us, via a job and a paycheck. Therefore, the taxes we pay are a symptom of His provision, in our modern world under our current governmental system.

If we pay taxes, this means that God has entrusted us with some level of His resources, and He is giving us the opportunity to steward those resources with care and wisdom. This, my friend, is reason to celebrate. It is a true gift to be entrusted by God with His precious resources.

A truth that I think is sometimes overlooked in our church culture today is the fact that God gave mankind work—the gift of creative productivity—in the garden of Eden, before the Fall, before sin came.

We know that we are made in God's image, which means that having the opportunity and ability to work is a means of expressing God's image in us. Work is stressful and can be an uphill battle because we live in a broken world. However, work is a beautiful gift that, when exercised, is a means of expressing God's image to a hurting and needy world. Your work is just as much a stewardship opportunity as your money. Because work, income, and taxes go together, paying taxes provides a great opportunity for us to remember the value that God places on work and to be grateful to God for His provision of work in our lives.

> Paying taxes provides a great opportunity for us to remember the value that God places on work and to be grateful to God for His provision of work in our lives.

All Government Is God's Government

In my years of studying the Bible, the most straightforward passage of Scripture that teaches about our posture toward the government is Romans 13. In it, Paul strongly exhorts the Roman Christians to submit to the governing authority. Mind you, these are the very Romans who imprisoned Paul and later likely beheaded him. These believers weren't living in a friendly political environment!

You may be questioning Paul's main reason for teaching submission to the Roman authorities. Maybe he anticipated this same question from the Roman Christians because in Romans 13:1 he says, "There is no authority except from God, and those that exist are instituted by God." No matter what the government is doing—good or bad—the fundamental driving reason for being a good citizen depends on God's authority rather than on the government's action or inaction.

In our politically charged American system, we all have a voice and we love to exercise our voice on behalf of change. It is tempting to think that we should only have an attitude of submission and respect for the government if it is doing the "good" we deem appropriate at the time, according to our political beliefs. Paul's teaching says, "Not so." (I am not saying that when the government permits or sponsors biblically unethical actions that we willingly comply, but I am saying we should not apply this biblically unethical standard too broadly to government actions that we just don't like—like taxes.)

Taxes, in particular, are a hot button for many who are politically engaged and active. There are many, many places that the government spends our money. Some of those places do not align with our priorities or, more important, our values. Nevertheless, we are wise to remember Paul and his teaching about taxes.

> For government is God's servant for your good. But if you do wrong, be afraid, because it does not carry the sword for no reason. For government is God's servant, an avenger that brings wrath on the one who does wrong. Therefore, you must submit, not only because of wrath, but also because of your conscience. And for this reason you pay taxes, since the authorities are God's public servants, continually attending to these tasks. Pay your obligations to everyone: taxes to those you owe taxes, tolls to those you owe tolls, respect to those you owe respect, and honor to those you owe honor. (Rom. 13:4–7)

Whether government knows it or not, it is "God's servant." Public servants are, therefore (whether they know it or not), "God's public servants." Paying taxes is part of what we do to honor those in authority over us and to submit to the authority that God ultimately has put in place via our system of government and via the people who serve in our government.

So, for those of you who are politically active, I encourage you to honor those in government as fervently as you fight for the causes and platforms that you hold dear. Our children and grandchildren, especially, need to see examples of Christian men and women holding government and authority in high regard as they learn how to be wise, engaged citizens for the next generation.

I find that paying taxes gives me a chance to remember the blessing of living in a country that is safe and in a community that is well run. Of course, we can always find fault with the foibles of government and the policies of our elected officials, but when we drive on good roads, enjoy ready access to emergency services, visit a beautiful national park, or go to bed knowing we have a national defense that stands ready to protect and defend our country, we have an opportunity to reframe how we think about taxes and be grateful for the country and the government God has given us.

Don't Let the Tax Tail Wag the Dog

It often falls to financial advisors to integrate many different parts of a person's financial plan. When I was counseling clients, I really enjoyed aligning their various plans—their insurance plan, their cash flow plan, their long-term savings plan, their estate plan, and their tax plan—with their goals and priorities. This part of counseling people allowed me to help them step back and think about the big picture and work with them to fit their various "plans" into their long-range goals.

One of the main traps that I watched people fall into over and over had to do with their taxes. Many people would become financially nearsighted as they jumped at opportunities to reduce their taxes without taking into account the true cost of that tax reduction.

I will never suggest that we should pay more taxes than are absolutely necessary, so good tax planning is key. But, I'd like to caution that we avoid getting caught by the lure of tax reduction as a goal in our financial decisions. At the end of the day, there are only two ways to effectively and consistently reduce our taxes—we can reduce our income, or we can spend more on something that is deductible. It is my firm conviction that a prevailing cultural financial goal—tax reduction—needs to be replaced with the financial goal of freeing up more cash.

The question that most of us don't ask when we're considering a tax deduction is, "How does this decision affect my bottom line cash flow?" or "When whatever I'm planning to reduce my taxes is complete, will I have more cash flow or less?"

> A prevailing cultural financial goal—tax reduction— needs to be replaced with the financial goal of freeing up more cash.

Let me explain.

One of the most common traps of this sort has to do with mortgages. The conventional argument is that mortgage debt is a good thing because of the interest deduction. Frequently a homebuyer justifies taking out a bigger mortgage due to mortgage interest deduction. However, this rationale discounts the fact that the tax deduction is actually costly and may not really be worth it.

Take this scenario, for example:

Let's say Harry and Harriet Homeowner are in the 40 percent tax bracket, they pay $10,000 in mortgage interest every year. At the

40 percent rate, they get a $4,000 tax benefit . . . and that is a lot of money! (They plan to use their tax savings to go on a well-deserved vacation!) The Homeowners feel like this tax advantage is such a good deal that Harry and Harriet decide to move to a bigger home where they now pay $20,000 in interest every year, creating a subsequent $8,000 tax advantage (and a better vacation!). The "deal" keeps on growing, every time the Homeowners take out bigger mortgages for better homes.

But, in their excitement over new and bigger homes, Harry and Harriett (and their mortgage lender) are slow to remember that, in fact, every tax deduction costs something. For Harry and Harriet to get the $4,000 or $8,000 of benefits mentioned above, they are actually paying a net $6,000 or $12,000 in additional interest, beyond the portion covered by the tax benefit.

Harry and Harriett have dinner one night with their new next-door neighbors, Gene and Gina Giver. Over cheesecake, the Givers share with the Homeowners about their favorite charities and ministries, including an orphanage in Central America. The Givers know that Harry and Harriett are pretty well-off financially, and they see that the orphanage's story and outreach really speak to the Homeowners' love for children. The Givers go out on a limb and challenge Harry and Harriet to match a recent $10,000 gift that Gene and Gina gave to the orphanage. The Homeowners seem surprised by the challenge, and they leave without committing.

"Wow, that cheesecake must have some sort of secret ingredient for them to really think we could afford to donate $10,000 to that orphanage," remarked Harriett to Harry later that night. "There's no way that would be feasible for us—I just can't see making that happen in addition to our other obligations." Ever the optimist, Harry replied, "But Harriett, think of the tax deduction—we'd get $4,000 of that money back, effectively, wouldn't we?" Harriett looked at Harry across the bathroom and said, "Seriously, Harry, where will we find even $6,000 to give? We can talk about it, but that's just a huge amount of money to commit in one lump sum like that, no matter what the tax advantage would be!" Sighing, Harry relented, "I guess you're right, but it was fun to imagine being wealthy enough to give like that, wasn't it? I really wish we had money to give like the Givers do. That must be really something!"

The Givers and the Homeowners are experiencing the exact same tax benefit. In the case of their mortgage, the Homeowners feel like their deduction is a "deal"—helping them get more house for effectively less money. In the case of the charitable deduction (which works the same way as the mortgage deduction), the Homeowners feel that giving a large sum is just out of reach—a goal that may be fun to consider but is really too costly.

These $10,000 examples are the exact same, financially speaking. They both cost the couple the same amount, and they both benefit the couple the same amount (assuming they are in the same tax bracket).

For the Homeowners, it looks like this:

$10,000 in mortgage interest, paid to the bank

- $4,000 in tax benefit via the mortgage interest deduction

$6,000 actual cost (cash flow reduction) to the Homeowners

For the Givers, it looks like this:

$10,000 in charitable donation, paid to the orphanage

- $4,000 in tax benefit via the charitable gift deduction

$6,000 actual cost (cash flow reduction) to the Givers

Tax deductions cost both the Givers and the Homeowners real cash money—$6,000 each—in fact.

I am not at all saying that we shouldn't have mortgages or take advantage of the mortgage interest deduction. Home ownership can be a great thing, and the mortgage interest deduction helps to make it more affordable.

However, what I am saying is that reducing taxes always costs something. There's a prevailing cultural assumption that the tax impact of a mortgage makes home debt more "okay," but we need to be very, very careful with this idea. In reality **all** debt costs us something and **all** tax deductions cost us something, too. As my dad used to say, "There ain't no such thing as a free lunch." He was right. Don't fall victim to the counterintuitive trap where we plan to reduce our taxes but fail to count the cost of reducing those taxes.

I believe it is a gift to live under the authority of a government that offers tax incentives to encourage us to put down roots with home ownership, to give to people in need, and to save for the future. However, in every case, it's

Reducing taxes always costs something.

161

important for us to grapple with the real cost of taking advantage of the tax benefits we are afforded as Americans.

Taxes and Giving

Charitable giving is powerful in so many ways. As we have learned, giving makes sense for reasons much bigger than tax deductions, because giving breaks the power of money. When I give, my money becomes others-centered rather than being me-centered. The tax benefit is an added financial incentive to give, and understanding how to use it well is a part of good stewardship.

As a planned, regular giver, it is wise to consider giving via a "donor advised fund." I love my donor advised fund even more than I love my coffee. (You get the idea.)

A donor-advised fund is a philanthropic tool that many financial organizations have in place. Companies like Schwab, Vanguard, Fidelity, National Christian Foundation, Waterstone, and more, make it possible for us to give in lump sums (many have very low minimums to open a fund) to one place. We effectively can funnel all of our giving money to the fund and then assign it out to various ministries and charities, over time, either on a recurring basis or as we become aware of need. The donor-advised fund is, for all practical purposes, a "bank" for giving, managing, and assigning money out on a regular basis to the various charities we have chosen, per our instructions.

Christian funds, such as National Christian Foundation or Waterstone, ensure that their funds will always be used for Kingdom-oriented purposes, thereby protecting donor intent. Secular funds have less restrictive filters on donor intent and usually permit giving to any charitable or philanthropic organization.

There are multiple benefits to this type of giving. With a donor-advised fund, Judy and I receive one tax receipt for our multiple gifts at the end of the year. We also love it because it allows us to give anonymously very easily, too.

There are experts available to advise on creative ways to give more than just cash. Over time, I've come to appreciate that one of the greatest tax reduction opportunities is to give away assets that have appreciated in value—things like stock, real estate, retirement plans, and more.

The big idea behind this strategy is that we can give away an appreciating asset while both experiencing tax benefit and blessing someone else.

As an example, let's say Gene and Gina Giver pay $50,000 cash for some property and it appreciates to $100,000. If Gene and Gina sell their property, they will have to pay capital gains somewhere in the 25 percent range, or $12,500, reducing their cash in hand to $87,500. This represents a net gain of $37,500.

Appreciated Property Value:	$100,000
Original Property Value:	- $50,000
Profit on Sale of Property	$50,000

25% Capital Gains Tax	- $12,500
Net Gain to Gene and Gina Giver	$37,500

If, however, Gene and Gina give their property to a ministry instead of selling it, they get a tax deduction for a $100,000 gift, reducing their taxes by $40,000 and avoiding the payment of any capital gains taxes. While the Givers effectively "lose" $10,000 by buying the property for $50,000 and getting a $40,000 tax benefit upon its transfer to the ministry, they also give $100,000 to a ministry. So, there's a $90,000 net gain, in total.

Tax Benefit to Givers, upon Sale	$40,000
Initial Investment in Property	- $50,000
Financial Impact on Gene and Gina Giver	($10,000)
Appreciated Property Value	$100,000
Financial Impact on Gene and Gina Giver	- $10,000
Net Total Transactional Gain	$90,000

While the Givers' donation does cost them something, the total benefit is powerful. They have been able to steward an asset by sharing it with an organization that will be blessed by it while recognizing tax benefit in the current calendar year because of their gift.

Wise financial planners and experts at donor-advised funds can help us discover how to give creatively, perhaps even giving assets we already possess while benefiting our tax situation at the same time.

Taxes and Saving

I am a big fan of contributing to a retirement plan that reduces my taxes in the short term to experience long-term benefit. If saving via a 401k or 403b reduces my cash flow by 3 percent or 4 percent a year, it's just fine because I am saving for the future **and** experiencing a tax benefit. This scenario is a win-win. It becomes a win-win-win when I work for an organization that matches my savings. Participating in a matching savings plan with an employer is one of the most foolproof and productive ways to save money!

Who Does Your Taxes?

Sometimes it seems expensive to pay a tax preparer, but if you and I have any complexity at all to our financial situation, we really need someone professional to take a look at our taxes. The cost of using a good tax accountant can be offset very easily by the benefit and wisdom they offer.

Proceed with Gratitude

Taxes are a fact of life, and they can seem like a real drag. But, when we view them holistically, our consideration of our taxes can lead us to ask really good questions about our lifestyle, our giving, and our saving habits. By engaging with the questions our taxes reveal, we are grappling with important issues in other wedges of our pie.

Maybe this is the first time you've thought about taxes from the standpoint of what they represent. Paying taxes from an honoring and grateful heart is a concrete way to show our heavenly Father that we are aware of His gifts—the gift of His provision and the gift of the government He's placed in authority over us. The next time you pay taxes, I challenge you to remember His gifts and proceed with gratitude.

Takeaway

It is possible for us to be grateful when paying taxes because we are reminded of both God's provision and honoring the authority of our government. How has God provided for your needs—financial and otherwise?

What resources does our government provide? As tempting as it is to find fault with the way the government spends money, I encourage you to ponder the blessings afforded to you by your government. Sometimes thankfulness is a choice, but when we choose to be thankful instead of resentful it can reset our perspective and result in genuine gratitude and joy.

10

Grow

I recently met a forty-one-year-old associate pastor who had paid off his home after fifteen years of working toward that goal. He and his wife made a lot of hard choices during that time. They gave up lifestyle desires. They endured the misunderstanding of friends who did not understand their motivation or their hard-core budgeting. They stayed in a smaller home as their family grew. They sacrificed *much* because they had a goal of being totally debt free.

Today, they have no mortgage payment. He told me that even though they knew that being debt free would provide a huge level of financial freedom and flexibility, they really had no idea the extent of that freedom.

The pastor and his wife now have tremendous flexibility when it comes to financial decisions. They love being able to be generous givers. They love serving in the church, and they are better able to raise their family on a pastor's income because they have no mortgage. They are less stressed and more available to the opportunities God brings their way today.

He told me, "Our friends thought we were crazy, but now when they see the freedom we have to give, they see it differently. We are free to give whatever we want to because we don't have that mortgage."

What are your goals and dreams?

Do you want to be able to have less debt? Do you want to provide something for your family down the road that you know they will need? Do you want to buy a second home? Do you want to be able to give more generously?

Stop for just a minute and think about a goal or dream that you have—perhaps some desire has surfaced as you've read this book. Maybe you've gotten excited by a vision of what could be in your financial life. Saving—the Grow wedge of your pie—will help you get there.

Key #3: The Pie: Grow

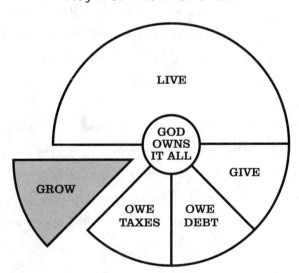

Grow: *Set long-term goals because there is always a trade-off between the short term and the long term.*

Remember that accomplishing any financial goal means spending less than we earn over a long period of time. We have to save, because to have it in the long term, we can't spend it in the short term.

Money Is a Tool

Money is not an end in itself; it is a tool to accomplish other goals and purposes. Many of our "goals and purposes" don't exist in the present; they relate to our future. The Grow wedge of our financial pie helps us to have the tools to handle tomorrow's worthwhile goals and purposes.

Sometimes we interact with our money as if it were a living, breathing thing that can control us. It may be humorous to imagine a "money monster," but the humor disappears when we fail to tame the money monster, giving it free reign instead of taking ownership to tame it and treat it for what it is: a handy and important God-given tool.

> Money is not an end in itself; it is a tool to accomplish other goals and purposes.

Solomon has a few things to say about wielding our money-tool well. In Proverbs 6:6–8 he says, "Go to the ant, you slacker! Observe its ways and become wise. Without leader, administrator, or ruler, it prepares its provisions in summer; it gathers its food during harvest." Ants are tiny, ruler-less creatures, yet they have the discipline to work today to care for the needs of tomorrow.

Solomon directly takes on people who are lazy toward money by calling them "slackers." He isn't messing around. Solomon is saying that we need to take responsibility for our relationship with our money—we need to prepare today's money for tomorrow's needs.

In Proverbs 21:20, Solomon reminds us that, "Precious treasure and oil are in the dwelling of a wise person, but a foolish man consumes them." When we tend toward consumerism, letting our appetite for "stuff" take over our financial decisions, we have effectively forsaken wisdom and joined the ranks of the foolish.

Saving money consistently means becoming disciplined. Discipline is always more effective when it has a few key ingredients: knowing the goal, establishing the habit, and having accountability along the way.

A Journey, Not a Magic Bullet

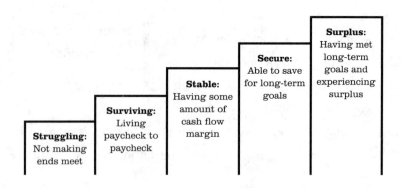

This chart helps us self-identify where we are in our financial life and decide where we want to go.[24] So where are you on the chart today? As you have examined your financial picture more closely, have you realized that you are struggling? Or, perhaps you've realized for the first time that you're much more stable than you thought. Maybe you realized that your financial reality is actually secure, freeing you to be bolder in living from your priorities.

Identifying our current location is an important starting point—everybody is someplace on the diagram. When we identify where we are, the first thing to grapple with is the question, "Am I content with where I am, or do I want to move to a different step?"

By the way, I'm not celebrating having a surplus as the ultimate goal. While I have observed that it is very stressful to be in the struggling category, I have also worked with very wealthy people who are extremely fearful and distracted due to their surplus. The fact is that every single position on the diagram comes with unique challenges and faith opportunities! Being content with what we have and setting faith goals to grow toward something different are actually very compatible realities, both of which depend on having an active, dependent relationship with the Lord at every step along the way.

The diagram represents a journey. Moving toward a stable, secure, or surplus level happens when, by faith, we apply the five simple biblical principles.

1. *Spend less than you earn* because every success in your financial life depends on this habit.
2. *Give generously* because giving breaks the power of money.

3. *Avoid debt* because debt always mortgages the future.

4. *Plan for financial margin* because the unexpected will occur.

5. *Set long-term goals* because there is always a trade-off between the short term and the long term.

Following these five wise money management principles is the only way to move to the right on the continuum—to take a faith journey from one step to another.

Where do you want to be in one year? Five years? Ten years? Do you have a dream to be on a different step in the future? If so, what is that dream?

The Sequential Investing Diagram

A sense of financial security is directly tied to savings. A Pew Research study recently showed that "a key reason Americans may feel financially insecure even though they rate their finances positively is that a majority (57 percent) said they are not financially prepared for the unexpected. In part, this reflects the fact that more than half (55 percent) of respondents reported just breaking even or spending more than they make each month, and one-third (33 percent) said their household has no savings."[25] The study also revealed that 83 percent of Americans worry about a lack of savings and 69 percent of Americans worry about not having enough money for retirement.[26]

I want to simplify a pathway to save for long-term goals, breaking it down for you, step by step. Remember that in the short term, we have only five uses of money—the five wedges of our pie. We simply must add money to the Grow wedge of the pie in the short term in order to meet any of our long-term goals. I know it can be confusing to consider various savings vehicles and options, but I want to reassure you that there are really only a few categories of savings goals, and there's a logical path from one to the other.

By prioritizing savings and by following the steps shown on the Sequential Investing Diagram, we can move into the stable, secure, and surplus levels where we have greater flexibility to meet future goals. Take a look at the diagram below. I've added key savings goals to each of the five steps on the way. As you read about the five levels of goals, think about where you are and what your next "Grow" step ought to be.

SEQUENTIAL INVESTING

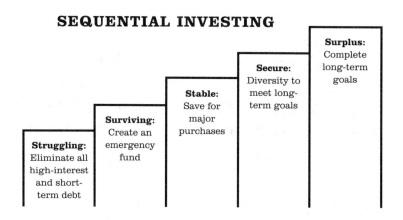

Step One: Eliminate all high-interest and short-term debt.

For those with consumer debt and other high-interest debt, the first and very best "investment" is to use any financial margin to pay it back.

Paying 15 percent, 18 percent, or even 22 percent in interest on short-term debt every month is letting the magic of compounding work against us. By spending less than we earn and paying off debt as rapidly as possible, we are effectively saving, or making an investment that automatically "earns" that high interest rate. This "investment" works because we will no longer have to pay the interest on the debt once it's paid, thus getting a guaranteed return equal to the interest rate we would have been paying. Making wise "Grow" decisions while we are in the struggling stage translates to paying off debt, because by doing so, we increase our ability to save in the future.

> For those with consumer debt and other high-interest debt, the first and very best "investment" is to use any financial margin to pay it back.

Step Two: Create an emergency fund.

Being in the surviving stage means that we are one emergency away from falling back into short-term debt. The very best way we can protect against this danger is to have an emergency fund. I recommend having at least three to six months of living expenses in a cash account, readily available, so that things like appliance repair, car maintenance, unexpected medical bills, or any other one-time unexpected financial event will not be catastrophic. Strategically speaking, after we have paid off all of our short-term and consumer debt in step one, we apply the same debt-repayment amount that we've been making to our new emergency fund until it grows to a healthy level.

Step Three: Save for major purchases.

A stable financial situation means that we are beginning to weigh our priorities and make choices about how financial margin will be used. An important way to be strategic is to identify major upcoming purchases and have the savings in place to pay for them when they happen. Like I mentioned earlier, Judy and I take this approach with cars. We plan for them, save for them, and pay cash for them. It works well to save in this manner for a child's education or for an addition on a home or even for a fun vacation.

At this point in the journey, we have not even entered the territory of investing. In each of steps one through three, our saved money is allocated for a certain purpose with imminent use, so we don't yet invest it in places of risk, where we could lose our saved money in a downturn.

Step Four: Diversify to meet long-term goals.

At the secure phase, we can begin to diversify savings into investment vehicles, because we are now saving to meet long-term goals that will benefit from the magic of compounding over long periods of time. We will really see our money grow by saving early and by saving consistently!

Consider a hypothetical scenario with two investors. Investor A, "Annie," invests $200 per month into a tax-deferred retirement account starting at age twenty-five. She does this until she is sixty-five. Investor B, "Benny," invests $400 per month toward his retirement into a tax-deferred account starting at age thirty-five until he is sixty-five. Both Annie and Benny earn a 7 percent annual growth rate, compounded monthly. Here's how they end up:[27]

	Investor A	Investor B
Contributions	$200/month starting at age 25	$400/month starting at age 35
Total contributions at age 65	$98,400	$148,800
Retirement fund value at 65 with 7 percent monthly compounding	$565,391	$528,222
Earnings	$466,991	$379,422

Benny never catches up to Annie in total savings even though he has saved over $50,000 more. Due to the magic of compounding—the exponential benefit of interest on interest—she ends up over $80,000 ahead. When we take advantage of the magic of compounding, we don't have to take a lot of risk over time to have a lot of money in the end. Annie probably couldn't have invested her $98,400 in a risky investment and had it turn out to produce $466,991. However, it was well within her capability to invest her money little by little and see it grow to that number over forty years. Investing in this way is a lot more about preservation than accumulation—we make our money by the income we earn, and our investments help us to save and grow that income so that it is also available for later.

Regardless of age, it is always wise to save for the long term sooner rather than later and to clearly define the long-term goals for which we are saving. I've found it helpful over the years to classify people's various long-term goals into six categories:

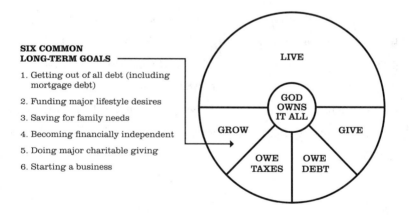

SIX COMMON LONG-TERM GOALS

1. Getting out of all debt (including mortgage debt)
2. Funding major lifestyle desires
3. Saving for family needs
4. Becoming financially independent
5. Doing major charitable giving
6. Starting a business

Reaching any one of these six long-term goals is easiest when we consistently save for a long time in an interest-bearing vehicle of some sort. In today's financial environment, finding a good financial instrument for long-term savings is relatively easy. There are many solid choices. I recommend using funds that have a proven track record of solid returns.

Step Five: Complete long-term goals.

When we are in the surplus category, we have met all of our long-term financial goals and we can "afford" to lose money. We can take greater risk, investing in new businesses or in higher risk instruments. I offer one word of caution here: an experienced, risk-taking kind of advisor is needed to help with this type of investing. Trying to navigate complex financial instruments or trying to assess changing market conditions is a full-time job, and it is wise to hire someone to help with this step!

For those on the path moving from secure to surplus, it is important to pre-decide plans for the money once we arrive at the surplus level. Deciding ahead of time helps us avoid the temptation to use money to buy more stuff or to give excessively to our children when they may, in fact, be harmed when we financially enable them rather than giving them their own opportunity to form good financial habits.

Biblically Wise Business and Investing

As we consider investing God's resources toward accomplishing our long-term goals, consider this: What are the moral and spiritual ramifications of our investments? This is an exciting time in the world of investing because there are some important developments reshaping this question.

Socially and Biblically Responsible Investing (SRI and BRI) are fast growing components of the investment universe. Two motivations are driving the trend: (1) Investors want to insure that their money is not going to support business activities to which they object. (2) Investors want to see their money advance causes that they believe would make the world a better place.

Not surprisingly, Christians are an important part of this movement. In fact, Christians started the first SRI funds. John Wesley's Methodist followers were among the earliest, followed by the Quakers who launched Friends Fiduciary in 1898 to manage assets in accordance with their principles of "peace, simplicity, integrity and justice."

BRI is influenced by Paul's teaching in 1 Corinthians 10:31: "Therefore, whether you eat or drink, or whatever you do, do everything for God's glory." God calls believers to do all activities to the glory of God, even the activity of business.

Consider that God is most glorified when His heart and character are reflected to the world, specifically His heart to love and care for His most prized creation: humankind. Jesus' call to "love your neighbor as yourself" is clear (Matt. 22:39). And business is one means of living out this call on a macro level.

How does God intend for business to be practiced so that it glorifies Him and points people toward a relationship with Him? Business can glorify God by loving and valuing the only part of creation created in His image: mankind. Business loves and values its neighbor by meeting material human need. When wealth is created and broadly deployed rather than hoarded by a few, businesses both alleviate material human problems and create economic provision. In both these ways, therefore, business can glorify God by providing a material foundation for human flourishing.

Sometimes businesses seek to primarily expand their own kingdom at the expense of their neighbors. One way this happens is through products that hurt people rather than help. A few examples would be tobacco, pornography, gambling, and abortion. Rather than fostering life, products can "steal, kill, and destroy" human flourishing.

Historically, the field of BRI has done a good job of highlighting these issues for its investors. As a result, many Christian investors have been exposed to the idea that one cannot please God by investing in **products** that God finds deeply displeasing. Yet, I believe that biblically wise investing should not only include avoiding products that steal, kill, and destroy, but also include investing in companies with God-honoring **practices**.

Businesses can violate "Love your neighbor" through bad practices, as well as through bad products. Case in point: there's nothing immoral about offering home mortgages to people who fall toward the poorer end of the economic spectrum. In fact, done conscientiously, this can bring real blessing to many. But in the aftermath of the great subprime mortgage debacle, it became abundantly clear that many companies sold these mortgages to customers whom they had every reason to know could not afford them and were virtually certain to end up losing their homes as a result. In other words, these companies harmed their neighbors by taking a perfectly acceptable product and exploiting people in the process.

BRI at its best helps investors put their money in companies that are creating compelling value for their various "neighbors"—customers, employees, and others. Companies where both products and practices further God's abundant life purpose.[28]

It is exciting to think that Christians can help to harness the power of their investments to advance God's abundant life purpose here on the earth. I would encourage you to seriously consider how your savings and investments honor God.

For those who are interested in pursuing a financial path that integrates issues of faith with goal setting, saving, and investing, I recommend finding an experienced advisor who shares your values. Judy and I wouldn't trade our trusted financial advisor for anything. He keeps us accountable; he guides us to ask the right questions in our decision making; and he walks with us through the various milestones of our life, each of which has important financial implications.[29] You don't have to navigate your financial decisions alone. There are amazing advisors around you—men and women who believe that their work is their calling and will walk with you as you integrate your faith journey with your financial decisions and plans.

Faith Goals

Whether we are just beginning to expand the Grow wedge of our pie, or whether we are seeking advice as sophisticated financial investors, having written goals is a key factor in moving from step to step along the Sequential Investing Diagram. As we grow financially, thoughtful goals motivate us and help us be wise with our financial resources.

There are volumes written about goals, so I won't belabor the topic, but I would like to mention an important and possibly new idea—setting faith goals.

Hebrews 11:1–3 says, "Now faith is the reality of what is hoped for, the proof of what is not seen. For our ancestors won God's approval by it. By faith we understand that the universe was created by God's command, so that what is seen has been made from things that are not visible."

Faith goals are different from normal goals. We set faith goals out of our conversations with God, knowing that His thoughts and His power are far beyond ours. When we set faith goals, we trust Him to lead us. God creates visible from invisible, and He wants to take us on a financial faith adventure.

The process for setting faith goals is quite straightforward. If you are married, you will participate with your spouse in the process, checking for unity at each step.

First, **spend time with God**, discerning His voice and His wisdom. Ask Him, "God, what would You have me to do?" about the financial situations that you are struggling with or planning for.

Then, **record your impressions**. Write, "I believe God would have me to _____." And then, ask, "Does this goal bring God glory?"

Next, **make that faith goal measurable and actionable**. For example, "I will allocate $150 per month to pay off debt by only spending $800 a month on food." This goal is measurable, by the month, and there's a way to make it happen—you can reduce your food budget for the family while you pay off your debt.

Finally, **act**. Faith requires action. As you act, your faith grows and your dependence on God's provision and grace is enhanced.

Goals can be scary because we fear failure or because we don't know where to begin with formulating goals. When we set faith goals, we rely on God and are able to act confidently. There's no need to focus on the past. Isaiah 43:18 reminds us, "Do not remember the past events, pay no attention to things of old." There's also no need to worry in the present. Ephesians 3:20 says, "Now to Him who is able to do above and beyond all that we ask or think according to the power that works in us." God has unlimited resources available to us. If He has given us a faith goal, He has the power to care for us along the way.

> The magic of compounding together with the power of setting faith goals greatly multiplies our financial possibilities.

Faith goals take us on a journey that can change with time, as God shapes our hearts and as He frees us financially. Living in a daily relationship with the Lord and holding our financial goals with an open hand allows our heavenly Father to speak to us along the way as He accomplishes His good purposes. In the end, having financial margin creates financial flexibility and freedom. The magic of compounding together with the power of setting faith goals greatly multiplies our financial possibilities.

Handle with Care

As with every other wedge of the pie we've discussed, the Grow wedge reveals heart issues: common temptations, and opportunities to practice trust and contentment as well.

When you see the word *saver*, does a specific someone come to mind? Does someone different come to mind when you hear the word *spender*? It is easy for the natural "savers" to think of themselves superior to the natural "spenders." Personality-wise, these types represent two ends of the spectrum! When these tendencies in us run amok, spenders tend toward the heart problem of materialism and savers tend toward the heart problem of idolatry. Saving can begin to consume us when we falsely believe that our money will help us attain our own safety, security, and future well-being. Legalistic saving—guarding money as though our lives depended on it—leads us into the dangerous heart territory of making money our idol.

I am amazed by television shows about extreme hoarders—people who accumulate trash or let their homes pile up with junk until the floors aren't visible. Most of us can't imagine living this way, but we may be inadvertently acting like hoarders when it comes to money. There's a fine line between saving and hoarding. To discern our own hearts on this matter, a good question to ask is, "For what am I saving?" If we are saving just to accumulate, we are probably hoarding. We are likely letting fear control us. Becoming rigid about savings can be an indicator that our security is rooted in our money.

Years ago I visited with a couple who had recently sold their business for $6 million. The wife wanted to replace a dresser that they had owned for their entire thirty years of marriage, and asked me whether they could afford to get a new one. Her husband had already refused her request. He did not believe they needed a new dresser because the old one was "just fine." In talking to them, I asked the man, "Are you willing to invest the price of a new dresser in your wife?" When I asked this, I could see the lightbulb come on for him—he realized that his tight financial control was actually having adverse relational effects. It helped him to understand that he wasn't parting with money just to buy a dresser; rather he was making an investment in his wife. You may read this example and think, *Wow, that's extreme!* but I have seen many times that people become blind to the fact that their concern with saving or managing their money down to the penny creates a significant relational hindrance. Remembering that money is a tool (and often a relational one!) is so helpful when we've closed our fingers around our money, grasping it tightly.

Another caution with saving is becoming intent on our saved money being used *only* for the purpose for which we saved it. When we have saved for one particular thing, it does not make it wrong to, in the end, use that money for some other purpose. More than once I've saved money for one thing only to use it down the road for something completely different.

I've found that a helpful paradigm shift to share with people struggling is what I call "provision versus protection." God calls us to *provide* for our families, being wise and planning ahead, but He is the ultimate protector and can be trusted as such. We can never save enough to *protect* ourselves from all financial eventualities. When we cross from providing to protecting, thinking that our money will be our ultimate shield in life, we have crossed into territory that God has promised is His—our ultimate well-being.

Ironically, it seems that people with the most money struggle the most with these issues. Wealthy people often are most cautious and careful to protect themselves from all circumstances that could threaten their finances instead of holding their money with an open, trusting hand, remembering that God owns it all.

There are so many powerful heart lessons that the Grow wedge can help us learn. We can learn to have a long-term perspective. We can cultivate the self-discipline required to save. We can experience a faith-journey with God. We can remember the true Protector of our future. Ultimately, through the Grow wedge of our pie, we can learn to exercise excellent stewardship, positioning today's resources with tomorrow's God-given goals and purposes in mind.

Takeaway

What is your next step on the Sequential Investing Diagram? Would you like to be in a different place than where you currently are?

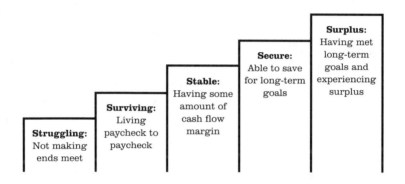

After you've identified your position, spend time working through the faith-goal-setting process to determine, alongside your heavenly Father, what actionable next steps are best for you to take to move to the next step on your financial path. The ultimate goal may not be getting to the fifth step, but until you know where you are going, you will never know when you arrive! To determine where you are headed, follow these faith-goal-setting steps.

1. Spend time with God.
2. Record your impressions.
3. Make your goal measurable and actionable.
4. Act.

11

Transformed Heart, Transformed Money, Transformed World

We have covered a lot of ground together. Thank you for joining me.

Over forty years ago, when I embarked on the journey of discovering what God had to say about money, I really had no idea what an adventure the learning process would entail. I could not have imagined all the people I would meet, the stories they would tell, or their Kingdom impact. Becoming a biblical financial advisor has also afforded me a front-row seat to God's work of redemption and restoration in and through people's lives in ways I could never have dreamed.

Prior to this journey, I never imagined the freedom, transformation, and renewal that can come from embracing God's truths and God's reality about money. Over these past several decades, I have seen men and women alike grow to where they began to think, act, and communicate differently about money. This change has transpired from the inside out as they have . . .

- *Lived as stewards, believing the reality that God owns it all.*
- *Surrendered their dependence on money for success, security, or significance.*
- *Allowed God to solve their money problem by first aligning their heart more closely to His.*
- *Answered the question of "How much is enough?" with a shift in perspective from thinking their resources are "never enough" to believing their resources are God's perfect provision for right now.*
- *Given generously, watching God do powerful things in their life and in the life of the receiver.*
- *Walked in faith, boldly pursuing God-given financial goals.*
- *Communicated freely in marriage, coming to unity in their beliefs about money.*
- *Taught their children to hold money with an open hand, delighting in the possibilities of biblical financial stewardship.*

When people are surrendered to God and following Him in their financial lives, amazing things happen. The smallest seeds of faith grow to bear fruit of great impact, far beyond what the obedient, surrendered steward could have imagined.

Salt and Light

You may have opened this book hoping for a quick fix or a trusty "how-to." If so, you may not have found what you were looking for, and that's okay from my perspective because I hope you discovered so much more.

I hope you found, instead, a new way of thinking—new perspectives and paradigms about who God is, who you are, and how God can use money in your life and around the world.

I hope you found trustworthy biblical principles to help you make wise decisions on this road of stewardship. I hope your toolkit has a few new reliable processes—like the Live, Give, Owe, Grow pie chart and the Sequential Investing Diagram, for starters.

More than anything, though, I hope you have a new, compelling vision of money as being so much more than a complicated medium of economic exchange. I hope your vision of money has expanded so that you understand it as a transformative tool that God uses first in your heart, then in your life and in the world at large.

Matthew 5:13–16 in *The Message* says,

"Let me tell you why you are here. You're here to be salt-seasoning that brings out the God-flavors of this earth. If you lose your saltiness, how will people taste godliness? You've lost your usefulness and will end up in the garbage. Here's another way to put it: You're here to be light, bringing out the God-colors in the world. God is not a secret to be kept. We're going public with this, as public as a city on a hill. If I make you light-bearers, you don't think I'm going to hide you under a bucket, do you? I'm putting you on a light stand. Now that I've put you there on a hilltop, on a light stand—shine! Keep open house; be generous with your lives. By opening up to others, you'll prompt people to open up with God, this generous Father in heaven."

Money is one of the most profound mechanisms by which we can bring out the God-flavors and the God-colors of the world.

Let me explain. Salt slows decay. Light reveals a good path. You, my friend, are salt and light. What you believe about money and how you use money can slow decay in this world and can light a path for others who are struggling to see.

> Money is one of the most profound mechanisms by which we can bring out the God-flavors and the God-colors of the world.

So what does it actually mean to become salt and light? Being salt and light can take many forms, but I believe that it means being people with well-formed personal convictions, walking wisely in a world that often elevates the unwise, and interacting with the world in a way that draws them to the grace and life that is found in Jesus. This book has given you an opportunity to consider, decide, and stand firm on your own personal convictions about money. When we become men and women of conviction, led by faith, we also become salt and light in the world—bringing out the

God-colors and flavors as we interact with our families, our friends, and our neighbors.

A couple of ordinary yet outstanding families come to mind when I think about salt and light—the power of personal conviction that defines a confident, surrendered steward.

After speaking at a ministry fund-raiser years ago, Jim and his wife, Jill, asked if I would meet with them one-on-one. They were interested in processing whether they could give more money away. At the time, their daughters were grown and Jim and Jill were living their empty-nest years in a very, very nice trailer park. Clearly, they could have afforded more, but their well-appointed trailer was enough for them in that season. As I looked at their numbers, I was easily able to reassure them that they had done a good job of providing for their family and for their own future financial needs. Giving more away was indeed feasible for them, so I helped them plan how to give more generously.

For thirty years, Jim and Jill gave more, all the while remaining clients of my financial planning firm. Not long ago, Jill contacted me to let me know Jim had recently passed away. She also wanted me to know that they had not only fulfilled their initial giving plan, but that they had given far more than they had ever hoped. She was kind to make sure I understood she was grateful for my assistance in helping them plan and be bold with their giving.

As I reflected back on their family, I was reminded of their profound contentment, their confidence in following biblically wise principles, and (perhaps most notably) the tremendously deep level of communication in the family—between Jim and Jill and with their daughters. Transparency of relationship and honesty about money did not constrain them. Their family was an open book, living out of firm personal convictions. They wanted to give more, and so they did.

Dois Rosser and his family also come to mind when I think of ordinary and outstanding. Dois Rosser is an entrepreneur I heard speak some years ago. He was a successful entrepreneur who had owned and sold several car dealerships. After he retired, he believed God wanted him to take the gospel to the world through the multiplying influence of church planting. Out of his wealth, Rosser started a ministry that has planted over four thousand churches in fifty-eight countries worldwide.[30] Of course, the vast reach of this man's vision and generosity struck me. I have found it to be the rare wealthy entrepreneur who is willing to give so freely and boldly. But the thing that stood out to me most was Rosser's adult daughter joining him on stage to take questions from the audience. Someone asked her, "Do you ever resent your dad giving away your inheritance?" Her answer was profound. She easily replied, "I've never, ever thought of it as my money." Clearly this family had a deep, pervasive conviction that God owns it all. Such a level of trust and communication about money is rare, and even more so in families of great means. The Rosser family's conviction that God owns it all both unified and freed them to do profound things for the sake of the gospel.

Money doesn't have to hinder us—whether we have a little bit or a lot. Practicing contentment and following biblical principles about money can free us as well as future generations in amazing ways.

Never Enough

There are many more stories about transformed lives that I could tell. Stories that would inspire and encourage you. But I know that many of us continue to live in financial fear, discontentment, and confusion. Why is that? Why do so many of us wrestle with the sense that there's "never enough"?

The title of this book speaks to the vague, gnawing sense that there has to be more and that money is the answer.

This struggle—the financial tightness that many of us really, actually feel—is powerful. It's distracting. It's defeating. It's frustrating. It's pervasive. For some, the struggle causes us to obsess over financial minutia and argue with those we love. For others, the struggle causes us to throw the budget out the window and take ourselves out for a nice dinner to forget our financial woes . . . only to be hit with them when the low balance alert e-mail comes.

The reality is that, for all of us, financial struggles call for permanent, new ways of thinking that will equip us to make wiser decisions on a daily basis. We've learned a lot together and our gained understanding can begin to impact us for the better as we begin to implement biblical financial wisdom.

You now know that perspective changes everything. When we understand that God is the owner and we are His stewards, we can be content.

You now know that there are only a few key financial principles to apply each day in order to produce financial stability in the long term:

1. Spend less than you earn
2. Give generously
3. Avoid debt
4. Maintain financial margin
5. Set long-term goals

You now know that there is only one pie and that when we follow biblical wisdom as we Live, Give, Owe, and Grow, we are able to practice contentment in our finances on a day-to-day basis. You know that the normal, cultural priority order of money, where we let the Live category yell the loudest and gain the most attention, is not actually the wisest priority order of money. You now know that there is a better way. You know the wisdom of moving the Live category to the bottom of the priority order, freeing up the Give and Grow categories and wrestling with the very important question in our Live wedge: "How much is enough?" You know the wisdom of eliminating debt in the Owe wedge and you know that paying taxes with gratitude is a way to honor our heavenly Father—the source of our earthly provision.

In most of our financial situations, we have enough. Enough is a choice and a mind-set. In any financial situation, contentment is possible. We are foolish to believe that "more" is always the answer.

Together, let's proclaim, "Enough is enough!" and begin to be people who are marked by deep contentment and who are known for living according to their convictions.

Personal Convictions

In my work with advisors, I train them to counsel their clients from a biblical perspective. I teach them much of what I've shared with you.

Here is the specific challenge that I leave with each advisor: You cannot take a client where you have not been yourself. If an advisor is trying to share biblical financial wisdom with a client and the advisor is not willing to put into practice the principles they are sharing, their advice will lack power and depth of insight.

Similarly, I'd like to conclude our time together by challenging you to think about your personal convictions. As you have read, holding your financial reality next to biblical financial wisdom, have you been convicted? What do you sense God asking you to know, believe, or do differently than before reading this book? Where is the current "rub" in your finances?

Your heart is there in the middle of the "rub" too, you know. If we've covered anything, we've covered the fact that our hearts and our money are deeply linked. The treasure principle—"for where your treasure is, there your heart will be also" (Matt. 6:21)—goes hand in hand with Proverbs 4:23 which says, "Guard your heart above all else, for it is the source of life." When we become convinced that God is leading us—whether He wants to bring a financial desire to fulfillment, whether He wants to transform a financial conviction to a habit, or whether He wants to bring a financial struggle to conclusion—we are wise to fiercely guard the lesson He is revealing. We are wise to own it and pursue it, knowing that learning His lesson is a means by which our hearts will be transformed.

> What personal conviction, applied consistently and thoroughly in your finances, would change your financial picture and cause your life to be salt and light to those around you?

So what is your "main thing" today? What personal conviction, applied consistently and thoroughly in your finances, would change your financial picture and cause your life to be salt and light to those around you?

Know, Believe, Do

I believe that every personal conviction moves through three layers: from "know" to "believe" to "do." I first know something in my head, I then come to believe it in my heart, and finally I do it—I act it out in my life.

198

The beauty of walking with God as a steward is that He takes each of us on a unique "know, believe, do" journey. When we move from knowing to believing, we are choosing to trust God and to take Him at His word. Sometimes this emerging trust involves a journey that begins small and grows stronger as our faith expands. Then, as we move from believing to doing, our convictions become action. We walk more and more boldly in the path that God is revealing to us.

Tim's Journey

Tim knew he was bored at work. He'd been a financial advisor his entire career, and helping people guard their money as if their life depended on it no longer energized him. One day, Tim called Todd, his best friend from high school, and asked Todd if he was bored at work too. Todd said, "No." Todd worked with a ministry that helped people understand and apply generosity. He explained to Tim how the work was actually very engaging and never boring. The idea appealed to Tim, and Todd soon invited him to leave his advising career to join the ministry—definitely not a boring proposition! As part of the process to determine whether God was leading his family in the direction of full-time ministry, Tim and his wife began to live at the level of a ministry income for a few months—they wanted to practice living on less. This experiment became a joyful habit as they realized that they had "enough." They discovered the freedom to be more generous. They discovered the power of contentment. Tim decided not to join Todd in ministry. Instead, he discovered a new passion for helping his clients answer, "How much is enough?" and helping them learn to live more generously. He had known biblical teaching about money, but when this season of wrestling in his career led him to activate his knowledge into belief and then into action, his heart was transformed in the process and his passion for his work was renewed.

The Meloon's Journey

In the late 1950s, the United States government pulled a contract for several hundred boats from Correct Craft Boats, forcing the layoff of hundreds of workers and eventually leading the company to bankruptcy.[31] Walt and Ralph Meloon, whose father founded Correct Craft Boats, had a strong personal conviction about debt. They believed that they had a moral obligation to pay back their creditors, even though their debt had been "erased" via Chapter 11 bankruptcy. The family spent nearly twenty years finding every creditor and paying back what they borrowed. The Meloons' commitment even meant that they spent a season of time living as a family in a tent at a campground in order to honor their word. In the end, they tracked down the very last creditor and discovered that she was in the hospital, very much in need of the financial provision their payment provided. They rejoiced that they were able to pay her back and meet a real need in her life. Ralph's family took "do" to a whole new level because of their firm belief that God was calling them to pay all of their debts back. Today, their business is thriving and they have set an example of integrity beyond what most of us could even dream about.

Pam's Journey

Pam had been a financial advisor for many years. She guided clients in investment and real estate decisions but had never heard someone teach about a biblical priority order of money. A few months after she went through a divorce and became single again, Pam's pastor challenged the congregation to spend their money in a new order—give first, save second, spend last—for thirty days. Pam accepted the challenge and said this of her family's story of transformation:

> That message was my big turning point. After I left church that day, I was excited to give it a try for thirty days. It was God's invitation to get involved in my finances. I was just starting to get a handle on what I owned and on the income that would be coming in, so the challenge came at a good time. I sat down with a spiral-bound notebook, looked at the amounts, and set our number for giving, our number for saving, and the remaining number was designated for us to live. I had a family meeting with my girls, ages six and ten. We talked and prayed together and committed to give it a try. After we put the numbers on paper, we wrote our giving check. It was a real stretch, but we were excited to try this. Then, we moved our savings number over to the savings account. After a month, the habit was set; God met me in our financial prioritization and I never looked back.

Pam's "know, believe, do" journey was crystal clear that day. The pastor's teaching resonated with her, helping to crystalize her personal conviction to prioritize generosity. The simple "give, save, spend" model provided a template for budgeting during the season in her household when she was the sole breadwinner. Over the years, Pam and her daughters developed the habit of meeting annually about the family finances. They began their meeting by setting personal goals and family goals, and then they planned how they would allocate their money to meet those goals, always starting with give and save first, then budgeting within their spend category. Pam says, "There were times when I had to sell an asset or look for additional sources of income—the plan required action on my part. But it has been very livable. Taking that one step transformed how I handled money. It charted the course for the next decade of my life. Trusting God first with my finances was the smartest decision I could have possibly made."

I could go on and on with stories of people who gained knowledge, allowed it to permeate their hearts, and acted on it boldly in faith. Men and women like Tim, Walt, Ralph, and Pam are those who go from "know" to "believe" to "do." These types of men and women willingly enter into a transformational heart/money journey. They become transformed, trusting God to train their hearts toward abundant life as He trains their finances toward deeper levels of stewardship.

We all have a choice.

Will we let money cover up our heart issues or will we allow God to use money to reveal and change our hearts?

When our hearts are changed, the world around us is blessed. The world has the opportunity to interact with contented, confident families who aren't afraid of or controlled by money. The world has the opportunity to interact with families who know the Owner of all things and who take Him at His word. The world sees God-colors and tastes God-flavors in new and exciting ways.

A Transformed World

Certainly this transformational journey of biblical stewardship frees us on a personal level. It also has the power to free the body of Christ on a corporate level. More exciting still, it can even free those outside the church by shining God's grace and love to the world at large.

In our country alone, I feel confident that we possess the resources that could offer healing to the world's deepest wounds and offer life to those who do not know the good news of the love of Jesus. We could fund the caring of orphans and widows. We could fund the mission work in our cities and around the world. We could provide resources for those who have been in need for generations. Resources are not the issue. Hearts are the issue.

> Imagine for a moment what the world would look like if Christians on a global scale were deploying God's resources according to His purposes.

Imagine for a moment what the world would look like if Christians on a global scale were deploying God's resources according to His purposes.

What if we believed God owns it all? What if we lived confident, intentional, financial lives where our decisions were rooted in biblical wisdom? What if the constant noise of money issues was quieted as we experienced contentment, confidence, and good communication? What if we had integrated our faith journey with our financial journey? What if our stewardship journey was also a transformational heart journey? What if . . . ? You complete the question and dream for a moment of the "what-ifs."

All of these possibilities are real. I've seen hundreds and even thousands of people experience them. They can be real for you.

So today I pray blessing over you as you go forward, acting in wisdom and believing that His truth is enough. Whenever I get the privilege of signing a book for someone, I always reference 2 Corinthians 8:9. I love the reminder of the ultimate, generous grace of Jesus, who makes us rich with every spiritual blessing. It's my honor to share this verse with you, praying that you will close this book with renewed financial hope, increased financial confidence, deeper financial contentment, and a powerful new faith in the Creator and Sustainer of all things.

> For you know the grace of our Lord Jesus Christ: Though He was rich, for your sake He became poor, so that by His poverty you might become rich. (2 Cor. 8:9)

Takeaway

I pray that God has been speaking into your life about how He wants to free you from your financial fears and lead you toward greater contentment.

Change almost always starts small. I am certain that if you pursue the one or two new habits or perspectives that you have gained through this book, you will see important, transformational change over time. God has an amazing journey ahead for you. Trust His leading and provision and move forward with confidence!

Blessings to you. Thank you for sharing this journey with me.

Notes

1. More on this idea can be found in Timothy Keller's book *Counterfeit Gods* (New York: Penguin, 2009).

2. Seen at https://www.youtube.com/watch?v=a_y5XpLUla0.

3. See https://generousgiving.org/media/videos/bill-vonette-bright -surrendering-everything.

4. A. W. Tozer, *The Knowledge of the Holy* (New York: HarperCollins, 1961), 1.

5. Dr. Gail Matthews from Dominican University of California recruited 267 participants to study how written goals, a plan for goal achievement, and accountability effect the completion of goals. The study found that the most effective way to accomplish goals is to write them, have a plan to achieve them, and have accountability in accomplishing them, http://www.dominican .edu/dominicannews/study-highlights-strategies-for-achieving-goals.

6. See http://www.cnn.com/2008/us/09/18/ike.last.house.standing/.

7. You can read the whole story of John Cortines and Greg Baumer in their book *God and Money: How We Discovered True Riches at Harvard Business School* (Carson, CA: Rose Publishing, 2016).

8. See http://www.lettersofnote.com/2012/12/america-is-like-that-second -kind-of.html.

9. As told by Graham Smith at the Generous Giving conference in Atlanta in 2014. Testimony found at http://generousgiving.org/media/videos/graham-and-april-smith.

10. Ibid.

11. See https://www.biblegateway.com/resources/commentaries/IVP-NT/2Cor/Guidelines-Giving for a more complete discussion of Old Testament tithes.

12. See https://generousgiving.org/media/videos/i-like-car.

13. As told by Rev. Brian Habig in his sermon, "A World Needing Justice," April 17, 2016, http://downtownpres.org/sunday/sermons/

14. See https://www.biblegateway.com/resources/commentaries/IVP-NT/2Cor/Paul-Sets-Forth-Guidelines.

15. See https://www.census.gov/people/wealth/files/Debt%20Highlights%202011.pdf.

16. See https://www.debt.org/wp-content/uploads/2012/11/Demographics-of-Debt.png.

17. See http://www.businessinsider.com/amazing-power-of-compound-interest-2014-7.

18. See http://www.huffingtonpost.com/2013/09/28/debt-mental-health-problems-depression-suicide_n_3997159.html.

19. See http://www.thesimpledollar.com/the-emotional-effects-of-debt/.

20. See http://www.huffingtonpost.com/2013/09/28/debt-mental-health-problems-depression-suicide_n_3997159.html.

21. See http://phys.org/news/2013-07-reveals-early-financial-arguments-predictor.html.

22. See http://www.thesimpledollar.com/the-emotional-effects-of-debt/.

23. See http://time.com/money/3684481/pay-off-student-loans-fast/.

24. This diagram is courtesy of Thrivent Financial. It is known as the "Five S Journey" and it is used as a planning tool with their clients.

25. See http://www.pewtrusts.org/~/media/assets/2015/02/fsm-poll-results-issue-brief_artfinal_v3.pdf, page 4.

26. Ibid., page 6.

27. This example was taken from Russell Investments. It can be found at https://russellinvestments.com/us/resources/individuals/planning-for-your-goals/starting-out.

28. Special thanks to Jeff Cave, Eventide's Director of Distribution, and Tim Weinhold, Eventide's Director of Faith and Business, for their contribution.

29. To find an advisor in your area who has been trained to offer biblically wise financial advice, visit www.kingdomadvisors.com.

30. Story found at http://www.cbn.com/cbnnews/us/2011/september/car-dealer-helps-plant-4000-churches-worldwide-/?mobile=false.

31. See http://www.thehighcalling.org/articles/essay/interview-bill-yeargin-ceo-correct-craft.

ACKNOWLEDGMENTS

From Ron

First and foremost I want to acknowledge my daughter Karen Guess who is the genius behind this book. She has spent years collecting all of the things that the Lord has allowed me to say and do and put them in a form that others can use. She is a gifted writer but more important a follower of Jesus Christ in every area of her life. Thank you, Karen; without you this book would never have been written.

I want to thank and acknowledge my son Michael who performed much of the editing and review of this book. He too is gifted beyond what his mother and I could have dreamed.

The scope and content of this book began in the offices of David Fincher and Scott Harsh at Greater Atlanta Christian School. They challenged me to think of a curriculum for high school juniors that would help them think biblically about money and money management. They had the faith to take what we came up with and begin to introduce it to junior students at GACS. Jessica Ly and Jordan House

211

were the two teachers who first began testing this content and gave terrific feedback and help in its development.

I want to thank two of my good friends. Mitch Anthony who challenged me to think about the uses of money in the construct of Live, Give, Owe, Grow; and Pat MacMillan who first encouraged me to think of all of our finances in a pie chart form, which made it much easier to view and understand.

I want to also acknowledge Larry Burkett, Howard Dayton, and Randy Alcorn. These three men have contributed so much to the truth that God's wisdom speaks to every financial issue of life and to all people. They have contributed much to the body of Christ that will only be seen in eternity.

I want to acknowledge four people whom I've had the privilege to walk alongside as God has worked over these last several years to give voice to His truth. Dr. David Wright is the president of Indiana Wesleyan University; Tony Stinson is the CEO of Kingdom Advisors; Rob West is the President of Kingdom Advisors; and Dr. Larry Lindsay, Chief Academic and Operating Officer at the Ron Blue Institute at Indiana Wesleyan, is someone who has become a very, very good mentor and friend.

Last and most important, my wife of fifty-one years, Judy, who has been a faithful encourager, counselor, and friend beyond what anyone deserves, most of all me. Thank you, Judy, for the testimony of your life to my life.

From Karen

To God, who established wisdom and saw fit to reveal it through His Son, and who empowers it in our lives through the Holy Spirit's work.

To my dad, Ron Blue, for the opportunity to distill the "core message" alongside you over the last eight years, and then for the gift of being invited to put it into words.

To the B&H team, for opening your doors and your hearts to this book.

To our agents, Robert and Andrew Wolgemuth, for being men of insight, dedication, and grace.

To Heather Nunn, for editing expertise and ongoing encouragement for this first-time author.

To Rob West and Tony Stinson, for kindly encouraging this book and for leading the way in passion about the advancement of biblical financial stewardship in every arena.

To Michael Blue, for partnering-in-crime, working on the finer points and the big picture with me.

To Beth, Brad, Pam, Tim, John, and Graham, for being willing to offer your stories as signposts for people on the journey.

To Kingdom Advisors, Generous Giving, ILikeGiving.com, and The Ron Blue Institute for providing inspiration and offering places people can go to learn more and to apply financial wisdom.

To the Bledsoes, for offering their cabin on the lake for the final push on the first draft.

To Doug, for being a steady, smiling spot in the ups and downs.

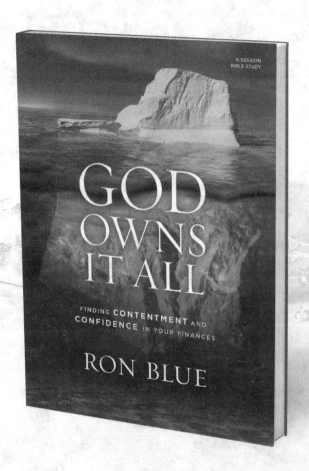

SHARE THE WEALTH

If you found value in this book, why not share its ideas with your small group? The six-session Bible study *God Owns It All* makes it easy. The *Leader Kit* includes two DVDs containing six 30-minute teaching sessions led by Ron Blue. Coupled with a *Bible Study Book*, each participant will learn to approach money management and financial planning with freedom, generosity, contentment, and confidence. Look for it in the Christian bookstore near you.